The Essentials of Tutoring:

Helping College Students Develop Their Writing Skills

by

Paul Gary Phillips

and

Joyce B. Phillips

HOUGHTON MIFFLIN COMPANY   BOSTON   NEW YORK

Vice President, Publisher: Patricia A. Coryell
Senior Sponsoring Editor: Suzanne Phelps Weir
Senior Development Editor: Martha Bustin
Editorial Associate: Anne Leung
Editorial Assistant: Jake Perry
Senior Manufacturing Coordinator: Marie Barnes
Marketing Manager: Cindy Graff Cohen

Printed in the U.S.A.

Library of Congress Control Number: 2002106555

ISBN: 0-618-43796-7

123456789-QF-08 07 06 05 04

Table of Contents

Preface

Whether a writing center serves students who need help with basic writing skills, or serves ESL level students, freshman composition students, or more advanced writing students, tutor training is indispensable for two reasons. First, training helps tutors gain confidence in general tutoring concepts, in verbalizing grammar concepts, in the writing process, in essay development, in research papers, and in tutoring non-native English speakers. Second, when tutors are well-trained, a writing center will be an excellent resource to help students succeed in their academic endeavors. The tutor training process starts with effective screening tools that not only help identify potential tutors who have good writing skills but also identify individuals who possess those special people skills so necessary in dealing with students in a one-on-one conference. Once tutors are hired, training can begin. *The Essentials of Tutoring* will help in this training as tutors review the foundations of grammar and writing. At the same time, this guide will aid them in sharpening the requisite skills needed to produce effective tutoring. The intent is to provide a "hands on" experience through discussion of tutoring skills as well as through practical advice and written exercises. This training can be accomplished in either a classroom setting or in a self-paced, self-teaching manner. In short, the aim is to show tutors how they can best help students succeed in learning the craft of writing.

This guide covers three areas. In the first section, entitled "Surveying the Tract," tutors will find material relating to the basics of tutoring— information about writing centers, conducting tutoring sessions, and tutees. In the second section, entitled "Building a Foundation," tutors will find material about the basics of the English language—parts of speech, sentence parts, grammar, and punctuation as well as important information relating to ESL students. In the third section, this guide will address the topic of "Constructing the Edifice"—in this case, the edifice is an essay. The third section will also focus on the writing process itself: prewriting, drafting an essay, the rhetorical modes, and the research paper. In addition, the final chapter will give tutors hints on putting all this material into practice. The chapter also provides three essays on which to practice tutoring skills.

As a quick reference, *The Essentials of Tutoring* will aid tutors during tutoring sessions especially when dealing with technical terms of the English language in a particular session. Developmental level students as well as ESL students are studying the language in concentrated detail. Quite often these

these students ask tutors specific questions regarding terms of usage, grammar, and the writing process. These students are working on daily assignments to learn the language, are studying for tests, or are in need of help as they write their essays. To aid tutors in helping these students, this guide will present material and explanations in simple terms that tutors can use when conferencing. As well, it will offer numerous charts and tables that can also be used in tutoring sessions. Besides presenting the "nuts and bolts" of grammar and the writing process, this guide will also provide some practical tutoring information and advice such as exploring the types of tutoring sessions a new tutor will encounter, explaining the difference between tutoring and proofreading, offering hints for successful tutoring sessions, furnishing a brief introduction to learning styles, and suggesting some hints for how to use this guide.

No work of this sort can come into being without the support and help of others. In particular, we would like to thank our colleagues at Grossmont College: Cathy Harvey, English Department; Homer Lusk, English Department; Linda Mitchell, English Department; and Virginia Berger, ESL Department, who all took time from their busy teaching schedules to read and comment on this book. We sincerely appreciate their insight and suggestions. In addition, we would like to thank Chuck Passentino, Grossmont College ESL Department, who not only offered many helpful suggestions as we wrote the chapter on tutoring ESL students, but also permitted us to adapt several tables from his own forthcoming textbook.

Since this guide is for writing tutors, we would like to thank Peggy Hartman and Jesse Roach, Grossmont College English Writing Center tutors, for providing their insight, comments, critique, and suggestions. *The Essentials of Tutoring* endeavors to present realistic representations of the experiences tutors may encounter, and our thanks goes to Fumie Nakamura, former Grossmont College English Writing Center Tutor, for contributing an international student's perspective. We are also indebted to our editors, Suzanne Phelps Weir and Martha Bustin, who shared our vision and helped to make this work a reality.

Paul Gary Phillips,
Professor of English and English Department Chair
Grossmont College, El Cajon, California

Joyce B. Phillips
Learning Assistance Center Specialist
Grossmont College, El Cajon, California

December 1, 2003

Section I

Surveying the Tract: An Overview of Writing Centers and Tutoring

Chapter 1

What You Should Know About Working in a Writing Center

Whether you have tutored before or are a new tutor, the job of tutoring is a rewarding experience and, from many perspectives, a highly enjoyable one. The interaction between you and your tutees provides a sense of accomplishment when you see them succeed. As tutees endeavor to understand grammar, mechanics, and the writing process in general; as they ask questions; as they share personal narrative essays; and as they share their research essays for specific classes, you and your tutees often develop friendly bonds and feelings of connection. It is rewarding for you to share in their learning experience and growth. Working in a writing center also affords the opportunity to meet fellow tutors, staff, and faculty. Providing welcome academic interaction and intellectual stimulation, these connections can develop into long-lasting professional bonds and friendships.

A hidden benefit of tutoring is that it can often strengthen your resolve to continue in a selected field of study or move into teaching or a teaching-related field. Because of the enjoyment afforded by tutoring, many tutors eventually seek a career in academia, often teaching English, literature, or ESL. In short, though tutoring can involve much work and training, it is a life-changing experience, helping a person to grow personally and professionally.

This gratifying and enriching job requires professionalism and the skills of giving verbal explanations and asking leading questions. Most tutors, when hired, are good intuitive writers, but a talent for writing does not always translate naturally to excellent skills in explaining those concepts to others. New tutors often need practical how-to advice and a review of writing concepts to better prepare them for verbalizing those concepts in meaningful ways to students.

The Essentials of Tutoring is designed to provide that how-to training for you, the tutor. When helping students on basic writing skills at the remedial or developmental level or when helping ESL students, this guide will aid you in tutoring the writing process and the basics of grammar and sentence structure. In addition, this guide will assist in tutoring the more advanced writer who may need help producing a well-documented research paper. Many of the suggestions throughout the book will aid you in helping advanced writers improve tone and style or fine tune an essay.[1]

The intent of this guide is not to replace a grammar book, writing handbook, or a book on the theory of tutoring. Rather, it is designed to prepare you for the job of tutoring students, both those who need help with basic writing skills and those who need more advanced assistance. Tutors are often hired when the semester starts and must be ready to work with students as soon as possible, often in a matter of days. While tutoring skills can be learned on-the-job, this guide helps bridge the gap between a newly hired tutor and a ready-to-work tutor. Though you can use this material in many ways, it can most readily be used in any one or in a combination of three ways:

- as a self-paced training program
- in a classroom setting or in a formal tutor-training class
- as a reference tool during the course of a tutoring session

The Essentials of Tutoring is meant to be an overview—a concise, quick reference tool dealing with the major areas of the writing process and grammar that tutors encounter daily. Some information is presented in bulleted lists designed for rapid reading and quick comprehension. Additionally, you will find fictional dialogues between a tutor and a tutee. These dialogues will present ideas on how to discuss, ask leading questions, and conference with students. Additionally, the "Helping students" sections as well as the "Practices" will facilitate the development of your skills. As you work through the practice exercises, you might take the opportunity to rehearse verbalizing the grammar concepts. Also, at the end of this book, you will find an answer key for the practice exercises.

Profile of Tutees

As a tutor, you will probably help tutees who come to a writing center from many different disciplines—history, sociology, business, or other areas—in addition to English. Despite this variety in student majors and areas of study, you will most likely tutor students who need help at the "basic skills" level, or tutor students who write at the "more advanced" level, or tutor students who fall somewhere in between. Some or many of these students will need help on grammar concepts, on the writing process, or on both; you may also tutor students who need help on more advanced writing skills or the research process. Students' reasons for coming to a writing center are numerous. You might work with students by

- brainstorming with them when they start essays
- evaluating an essay's content and organization
- addressing specific questions about mechanics, grammar, and punctuation

- answering quick questions about grammar rules, dictionary usage, in-text citations, or a works cited page
- assisting with grammar software if your center is equipped with computers

Sometimes students bring an already drafted essay to a writing center and say to a tutor, "I need some help. Can you fix the grammar and all the other stuff wrong with the paper?" The scope of this request is broad. Where do you begin when this kind of request is made? First, you need to determine the level at which this student is writing, and often that determination can be made by ascertaining the English class (if any) in which the student is enrolled or has last completed. Second, do you help the student on only basic level writing skills because the student has asked for help on grammar? Or do you help the student on sentence structure? Or is the "other stuff" actually a request for help on essay organization? Or do you help that student on skills that are more advanced?

In many community colleges or four-year colleges, students may write anywhere between two levels of writing. The basic and advanced levels of writing can be thought of as poles on a continuum. Students may write any-where along this continuum, so the categories of basic and advanced do not necessarily correlate that basic level students (determined usually from the class in which they are enrolled) only need help on sentence level proficiency or advanced writers only need help on improving tone and style. To give you an idea of the two poles at which students may write, the following general descriptions are offered of basic writing skills and more advanced writing skills.

Basic Writing Skills

At community colleges, four-year colleges or universities, or other writing center environments, many students visit writing centers because they need help with basic writing skills: essay organization and structure, grammar, and punctuation. Some need a brush up on these topics while others may turn to writing centers to receive greater remediation or developmental level writing help. In addition, many colleges reach out to students who are non-native English speakers, the English as a Second Language (ESL) students, who are advancing their understanding and use of the English language. Like their native speaker counterparts, these ESL students also need help with writing skills, especially on basic grammar. However, whether students are native speakers or non-native English speakers, all basic level students will need to know and practice the following skills:

- how to construct an essay with an introduction, a thesis supported by well-developed main points, and a conclusion

- how to provide clarity and unity by using the rhetorical modes and other patterns of organization
- how to emphasize crucial points and create interest by employing a variety of sentence patterns
- how to write an essay containing minimal grammar and punctuation errors

Advanced Writing Skills

Not all students need tutoring in basic writing skills. Some students are already good writers, but they want to acquire even more advanced writing skills. These writers seek help in

- developing tone and style to effectively present or defend a position
- using research to support their points
- incorporating analogy, figurative language, or personification
- writing critical analysis about literature, history, philosophy, or other subjects

Unlike basic writers who focus on the organization and structure of an essay (introduction, body, conclusion, and the use of organizational tools such as rhetorical modes), more advanced writers focus on logic, argumentation, voice, and tone. When students at this level write argumentative essays, they use critical thinking and meaningful research to effectively support a position. These writers have developed a command of essay structure and use that structure in a manner that is transparent to the reader. Their writing shows an awareness of audience, purpose, and thesis. At this level, structure is a tool that supports meaning. When tutoring the more advanced writers, you will facilitate the creative effort, identify weaknesses in logic, or help refine an otherwise fine piece of writing.

Profile of a Writing Center

Before launching into the training portion of this guide, consider the following overview of a typical writing center. Understanding how writing centers function will give you a better feel for the scope of the tutoring job.

What to Expect to See in a Writing Center

To serve students efficiently, a writing center may provide the following:

- resources for tutors' and students' use: dictionaries, thesauri, grammar books, writing handbooks, grammar handbooks regularly used as class-

room texts, and, perhaps, texts used in English composition and ESL classes
- copies of grammar exercises
- handouts of common grammar concepts
- handouts of the most helpful Internet sources for writing students
- copies of departmental outlines for composition courses and ESL courses
- a number of computers with grammar software, word processing software, and Internet access

Writing Center Staff

A writing center may be staffed with any or all of the following positions:

- student receptionists who direct students to tutors or to a writing center activity
- student workers who help students with computer operation
- tutors who have experience and expertise ranging from the peer level to the graduate level
- a faculty person who coordinates or directs the center; who acts as liaison between the administration, instructors, and tutors; and who establishes the academic philosophy of the writing center and steers the center's course
- a lab assistant or technician who handles the day-to-day operation of the writing center or handles the technical aspects of the computers

Writing Center Organization

A writing center is more than a room. It includes organizational tools that help support the services required. A writing center may have some or all of the following:

- an area where students check-in and are greeted by a writing center worker who can direct them to a tutor or to the appropriate writing center activity that will meet the students' needs
- a system (computerized or manual) for tracking student use of the writing center
- an area to organize and file the center's record-keeping and operational material such as an appointment book, printouts of attendance rosters, timesheets, or tutor schedules
- an area for items such as timesheets, personal notes, flyers, or memos
- an area to post communiqués for tutors, receptionists, supervisors, or instructors
- handouts, flyers, or brochures that specify the center's policies, services, and open hours; specify if the center provides tutoring by appointment or walk-in; and specify any time limits on tutoring sessions

- handouts covering such topics as grammar explanations and exercises, essay structure, rhetorical modes, citing sources, and researching via the Internet

This chapter has reviewed students' varying reasons for using a writing center and looked at some basic components of a writing center. In the next chapter, you will have the opportunity to learn specific tutoring skills and strategies in preparation for your work with students.

Chapter 2

The How-To's of Tutoring

Okay, it's a few days before the new semester starts, and you are training for the tutoring position in your college's writing center. You have always known that you are a good writer. Crafting the words, sentences, and organization of your essays has always been easy for you. Suddenly, fear grips you as reality sinks in. Next week, you will start tutoring students.

   The butterflies in your stomach start to flutter. How are you going to transfer to other students your enthusiasm for writing? In fact, have you ever seen papers written by students who have major writing problems? How are you going to explain concepts and organizational writing skills that have come so naturally to you? How are you going to explain all those technical grammar concepts to students: Coordinating what? Subordinating what? Conjunctive? Participles? What kinds of questions are students going to ask? By the time you finish this guide, you will be better prepared to answer the above questions and deal confidently with any type of tutoring session.

Types of Tutoring Sessions That You May Encounter

The types of tutoring sessions that may be encountered will be determined by the writing skills of students at various levels of need. Tutoring in a writing center is actually helping students learn more about writing. You might tutor students in some or all of the following ways:

1. **Help students who don't know how to start writing essays.** You might brainstorm topics, narrow topics down, or help them write short outlines.

2. **Help students develop a thesis statement.** Some students have already composed an essay but feel that the essay is missing something. Often that something is a lack of clear focus because of a weak or nonexistent thesis statement. Here you might work through the essay's organization and brainstorm possible theses that fit the main points. This activity may include clarifying main points and strengthening the introduction and conclusion.

3. **Help students with the content of essays.** You might review the basic components of a composition such as introduction, thesis statement, topic sentences, body paragraphs that provide strong support for thesis, and the conclusion. Additionally, you may work with students on a more advanced level of writing, such as argumentation, research papers, understanding how to avoid plagiarism, use of in-text citations and works cited, or other elements related to research papers.

4. **Help developmental and remedial level students with grammar in sentences, paragraphs, or short essays.** For these types of sessions, you might work with a student who needs help with a particular basic writing skill or with learning grammar and sentence level skills. You might help them with a few sentences, a paragraph, or a short essay. For these students, since you would be focusing on a particular area of writing or grammar taught in the classroom, you should become familiar with course content so that tutoring sessions with these students focus on pertinent material. Encourage students to put into practice in their paragraphs or essays the grammar concepts and writing skills being taught in their specific class.

5. **Help students with one specific grammar concept.** A tutoring session may focus on, for instance, helping a student with comma rules, with sentence fragments, or with understanding and identifying dependent clauses. If a student needs help with clauses, the session may involve such activities as identifying subordinate conjunctions and relative pronouns and then identifying dependent clauses in sentences taken from a textbook, a hard-copy grammar exercise, or a grammar software program. This tutoring session could also include having a student write several sentences and identify the types of dependent clauses (adverb, adjective, or noun clauses) in these sentences.

6. **Help ESL students.** These students may require assistance with such grammar skills as articles, prepositions, verb tenses, sentence structure, or other basics. Like other students, they may need help with organization and content of already composed essays, but their grammatical errors and their use of vocabulary may be more challenging. Likewise, the approach you use when tutoring an ESL student may be different than the approach used for a native English-speaking student. For instance, if a verb tense is used incorrectly, you may have to explain the use of a specific tense and its relationship to other words in the sentence such as time frame words like *since, until, before,* or *after.*

7. **Help students with personal statements.** This type of session may include assisting students with college or university applications and scholarship applications. Some students may not even know how to start a personal statement. In this type of tutoring session, brainstorm with students to draw out their thoughts relating to the topics to be covered on personal statements or applications. If students bring in personal statements that are somewhat composed, look for the main points or

important points required by the college application. In their personal statements, students should demonstrate a strong voice, use concrete examples, and strictly follow the guidelines of the application. Students should avoid gimmicks, but they should start personal essays with a hook to capture the reader's attention. The personal essay should give the reader a sense of who the student is, why the student is deserving of acceptance to the college or university over all other students, why the student would be a good addition to the university, or why the student is *the* person to receive the scholarship.

8. **Help students with other types of tutoring requests.**
   - essays for composition classes
   - research papers or formatting MLA in-text citations or works cited
   - analytical essays for literature classes
   - journal entries and reading responses
   - written assignments from classes outside the English Department
   - résumés

Any or all of these tutoring requests for help (as well as requests not described in this list) could be encountered in one day. The operative word is *help*; that is, when you tutor, you will be helping students learn more about the writing process, about grammar, about punctuation, or about the research process. However, while you will be helping students learn more about writing, you will not be editing or proofreading.

Tutoring Versus Proofreading

As a tutor, you may be asking, "Why do I need to know about grammar and all that stuff? My writing center doesn't do proofreading." That's right. Avoid proofreading students' essays to correct grammatical and other mistakes. However, to help remedial and developmental writers, you will need to know about the parts of speech, grammar, and basic sentence structure. Even though many writing centers advise tutors not to focus on proofreading, many students still walk into a writing center and expect their essays to be proofread. At this point, set limits. You might explain to the students your center's policy on time limits for sessions or explain that tutoring will include explanations about grammar concepts but will not include proofreading. After hearing the policy, students may determine that they actually want the focus on organization, thesis, and support in the essay, or they may want the tutoring session to focus on the sentence level issues of writing. If students still want the grammar reviewed, then help them learn the skills necessary to proofread and check their own grammar. Allow students to edit their essays themselves by

- identifying students' writing strengths and weaknesses
- demonstrating how to use a grammar handbook

- explaining grammar rules and then coaching students to find other similar errors
- showing students how to revise by checking for logical flow, cutting out wordiness, and using transitions

In a short time, most students should be able to identify the same type of errors. This concept is nothing more than the old adage: give a man a fish and feed him for a day; teach a man to fish and feed him for life. As Beth Rapp Young, in her article "Can You Proofread This?" states, "Helping a writer to proofread can be tremendously valuable when it is done for the purpose of teaching the student to find her own errors."[1]

The –*ings* of Tutoring: Five Steps to a Successful Tutoring Session

The steps in the tutoring process can be divided into five major categories. These categories—Preparing, Beginning, Employing, Remembering, and Ending—can be called the "-ings" of tutoring because they require active involvement. They give a pattern or rhythm to the tutoring experience.

1. **Preparing for the tutoring session requires that you**
    - Be on time for the start of your shift.
    - Gather all necessary resources for a successful tutoring session: name tag or name sign, dictionary, thesaurus, grammar handbook(s), pens, pencils, erasers, and tutor response sheets or other paperwork for tutoring session feedback.
    - Check the appointment schedule if the center provides tutoring by appointment.

2. **Beginning the tutoring session requires that you**
    - Greet students warmly.
    - Ask students the reason for their visits.
    - Ascertain the nature of assignments and level of the class assignments.
    - Explain what reasonably can be accomplished within time limits allotted by setting an agenda.
    - Fill out any necessary paperwork such as a tutor-response sheet.

3. **Employing tutor techniques during a session means that you**
    - Encourage students to actively participate in sessions. In his article "Setting the Agenda for the Next 30 Minutes," William J. Macauley, Jr., states: "If you intend to encourage a student writer to take responsibility

for writing, do so from the start of the session by asking him to tell you what he is thinking, what he wants."[2]

- Formulate leading questions to encourage students to analyze and critically think about ideas they want to communicate.

- Encourage students to do the thinking and talking in brainstorming sessions.

- Use any or all of the learning center's resources to help students.

- Read some or all of students' writing aloud. Be sure to read verbatim. Read all the words exactly as the student has written them including misspelling and incorrect word choice. Reading aloud helps students hear the way their words are typed and helps them hear their own errors. Reading aloud also helps more advanced writers hear the flow, tone, and voice of their essays.

- Provide words of encouragement for the areas of the essay that are well-written.

- Ask students tactful questions to clarify awkward or illogical areas within the content of their essays. These questions encourage students to think of additional or alternate ways of expressing information and ideas. It is okay to ask questions such as, "I'm confused. What do you mean here?" or "Is there a connection between the point mentioned in this sentence and the point you make in the next sentence?" Formulate comments and questions so that students will not sense overly negative feedback about their writing but sense that you are encouraging them to express additional thoughts and ideas.

- Encourage students to make all necessary revisions; avoid writing on their assignment or performing editing or proofreading.

- Provide students with explanations about grammar concepts to help them discover their own grammar weaknesses. Point out major or recurring grammar errors, but do not attempt to find all grammar errors. Let the student writer use the just-discussed concepts to identify and repair any remaining errors in his or her essay although some of these remaining errors might deal with concepts not discussed.

- Use grammar books as resources so that students will understand the value of grammar handbooks. Refer to the books often, and become familiar with the various sections. Many grammar books have tabbed sections so that information is easy to find. Study the index of a favorite grammar handbook to feel comfortable using the index to quickly find answers.

4. **Remembering hints for tutoring effectively and efficiently means that you**

- Set limits on the amount of help. Time constraints will help set these limits, but also, a student and you should set the focus of a session by agreeing that "together we will look at _____." For example, the student and you may limit the session to look at only the thesis and support of thesis. The goal of the session would be to make sure that all main points, explanations, and examples tie to the thesis and central idea and that the support does not veer away from the topic. In another instance, you might limit a session by agreeing to look at only sentence-level problems. If you look at only sentence level problems you might explain how to subordinate ideas if the sentences are choppy, explain subject–verb agreement rules if agreement is a problem, or explain shifts in tenses if the student has used both present and past tense.

- Allow students to maintain ownership of their own essays and give students time to vocalize their concerns and ideas.

- Avoid the "I must find all the errors" mentality. Always insist that students do their own thinking and writing. Overcorrecting, a strong temptation for any tutor, has occurred when a student leaves a tutoring session with his or her vocabulary radically changed, when the sentence structure in some parts of the essay seems more advanced than in other parts, when the voice or tone of the essay seems to shift throughout the essay, or when the student hears more of the tutor's ideas embedded in the content. Molly Wingate in "What Line, I Didn't See Any Line" provides additional indicators of overcorrecting. She states that "Hallmarks of having overstepped the tutor role include talking more than the writer, noticing that the writer appears distracted or uninterested, and finding that the writer is always choosing the tutor's suggestions."[3]

- Recognize the difference between proofreading and tutoring. Proofreading is looking for errors, grammar and otherwise, in a single essay. Students may hear by word of mouth or from instructors that the writing center is a great place to get their essays edited or proofread. Writing centers were first referred to as "fix-it" shops by Stephen M. North in his essay "The Idea of a Writing Center" when he stated: "It is because the agency that created the center in the first place, too often an English Department, has made it so." He continues by labeling some centers as "the grammar and drill center, the fix-it shop, the first aid station . . ."[4] In today's writing centers, faculty and staff must be sure that tutors are trained to help students improve their writing skills, not merely improve one essay through the process of "proofreading" only. As North puts it: "In a writing center the object is to make sure that writers, and not necessarily their texts, are what get changed by instruction."[5]

- Help a writer understand the concepts behind revisions. Talk the writer through the errors; explain where and how changes can be made; then, ask the writer to explain to you, in his or her own words, the concept being learned. Remember: the word *tutor* means a private instructor or one who provides special or additional help. Proofreading and editing are done to an essay; tutoring is done for a student writer to improve his or her knowledge or understanding of the writing process. The job of tutoring is not to help a student get an "A" on one particular essay but to help a writer improve his or her overall writing for all essays.

5. **Ending a tutoring session means that you**

- Review and plan. Save enough time to review with the student the progress made in the session and give the student some direction on the steps necessary to finish the essay.

- Close on a positive note. It is important for students to feel supported and helped by their visits to a writing center. Whether a session is challenging or rewarding, do your best to end on an encouraging and positive note.

- Say good-bye. Most writing centers have time constraints on tutoring sessions. If the student's agenda is finished in the allotted time, then simply say good-bye. Always thank the student for coming to the center, and, if possible, escort the student to the check out area. However, much to your dismay, time may have run out before the goals initially agreed to are completed. You may need to politely explain that the session must end. At this point, recommend another tutoring session if another session on the same essay is permitted in your center. Be sure to include the review and plan step.

Students' Learning Styles

You can better help tutees develop improved writing skills by understanding that people learn differently. Some knowledge of students' individual learning styles will help personalize tutoring sessions to fit the learning style of different students. Essentially, people learn through three avenues: Auditory (hearing), Visual (seeing), and Tactile/Kinesthetic (doing). In reality, you may not know a student's learning style at the first session, so incorporate as many learning styles as possible into all tutoring sessions.

- For auditory learners, read essays aloud so that these students can hear the flow of their words. By so doing, they may hear the needed changes. Read rules aloud from grammar books to facilitate their understanding of rules or concepts in question.

- For visual learners, as you discuss grammar concepts, be sure to write notes, use handouts, and use lists and tables in grammar books to help students visualize the information. Encourage these learners to write down all thoughts generated or concepts covered in the tutoring session.

- For tactile/kinesthetic learners, suggest that students do the writing during sessions and suggest specific grammar software, which could include music, sound effects, color, graphics, and movement. For tactile learners, keep tutoring sessions to a minimum time since tactile learners have difficulty sitting in one place too long. Do not be disturbed if tactile learners tap their feet, kick their legs, or pull at their hair while think-ing. This constant motion helps the learning process of tactile learners.

The more ways students can learn new information, the easier it will be for them to remember. So encourage learning through ways that enhance all three learning styles: reading aloud, writing of sentence examples, writing notes, looking at charts and tables, or practicing grammar exercises.

More Hints for Helping Students

In addition to the five "-ings" of tutoring and being aware of learning styles, consider the following suggestions gathered from successful tutors:

1. **Ways to create a positive image when you tutor**

   - Be tactful, patient, and friendly as you conference with students.
   - Speak with confidence.
   - Use encouraging words, and avoid negative sounding words.
   - Speak slowly.
   - Use simple-to-understand vocabulary.
   - Avoid facial expressions that could be misinterpreted by students. For instance, a student could negatively interpret a frown.

2. **Ways to enhance student learning**

   - Use all resources available to provide alternate explanations.
   - Help every student, no matter what the student's skill level.
   - Ask leading questions pertinent to the errors and revisions; don't lecture. For instance, if you notice that a student has not introduced a paragraph with a topic sentence, describe the function of a topic sentence and then say, "Let's read this paragraph aloud. Does the first sentence introduce the topic of this paragraph?"
   - Write sentence examples and notes to help explain grammar concepts. Remember some students may be visual learners, so written notes will help them remember these concepts.
   - Use questioning and summarizing to review with a student the concepts worked on during a tutoring session.
   - Use different colored pens or markers to highlight parts of speech or parts of the sentence. The use of color will certainly help visual learners; likewise, all students will be able to follow and understand material easier when important areas are highlighted with color.
   - Encourage students to make the written revisions to their essay.

- Become familiar with English and ESL course outlines and internalize course content related to those various levels.

3. **Ways to be professional**

- Avoid any situations that would put into question tutor professionalism.
- Keep the confidentiality of students.
- Avoid discussing students' writing capabilities with other tutors. Although it is good to review tutoring techniques for your own gain of tutoring skills, avoid discussing individual student's performance; instead, review and discuss generalizations involving tutoring skills.
- Avoid discussing with a student the potential grade for an essay.
- Avoid interpreting for a student why an essay received a particular grade or criticizing an instructor for giving a certain grade.
- Avoid situations where students complain or ask specific opinions about assignments, graded essays, or instructors.
- Encourage students to speak with their instructors if there are serious areas of concern in the writing process.

How to Use the Rest of This Guide

In the first two chapters, you have reviewed some basic knowledge of writing centers and the job of tutoring. In the balance of the chapters, you will encounter interactive help and practical advice in the form of

- a quick reference for topics concerning grammar, sentence structure, and punctuation
- hints for working with all students whether native or non-native English speakers
- practical hints to help students learn grammatical concepts
- written exercises for practice on the grammar concepts previously reviewed (with an answer key provided at the end of this book)
- suggestions for verbalizing concepts to practice tutoring techniques
- material on the writing process, the structure of the essay, and the research paper
- fictional tutoring dialogues

The fictional tutoring dialogues are designed to show you how to ignite student creativity and critical thinking by integrating questions into tutoring sessions. You can approach these dialogues in several ways:

- read through them silently in a self-paced study plan

- read them aloud in a group or classroom setting, and then discuss these dialogues with the group
- recreate these dialogues as a mock tutoring session
- create your own dialogues as well as tutor and tutee responses

A final section, "Suggested Readings and Bibliography," lists resources for more in-depth grammatical explanations and examples, supplemental exercise books, and online sites with exercises and explanations. You can also consult resources in your own writing center or resources in your English Department.

Take your time to work through this guide. It is designed to help you as a self-paced training program, as a guide to effective tutoring, and as a reference tool you can refer back to as needed during the course of a tutoring session.

SECTION II

BUILDING A FOUNDATION: SENTENCE LEVEL TUTORING AND HELPING ESL STUDENTS

Chapter 3

Sentence Building Blocks: The Eight Parts of Speech

This chapter, as well as Chapters Four and Five, reviews all the parts, or building blocks, that can be used to create sentences. These building blocks are

- the eight parts of speech
- subjects
- verbs
- phrases
- clauses

Introduction to the Building Blocks of Sentences

Students' understanding of grammar, sentence patterns, and punctuation starts with knowledge of the basic elements that build on one another to form a well-constructed sentence. These building blocks of a sentence start with the eight parts of speech: **nouns**, **pronouns**, **verbs**, **adjectives**, **adverbs**, as well as **prepositions**, **conjunctions**, and **interjections**. Along with identifying a word as a part of speech, students must be able to identify how that word or building block functions in a sentence. Single words—nouns, verbs, adjectives, or adverbs—form parts of a sentence, but also groups of words—phrases and clauses—form larger parts of a sentence. These parts of a sentence also have particular functions in that sentence.

Before moving to a discussion of the eight parts of speech and other sentence parts, review the following charts about "Functions in Sentences," "Parts of a Sentence," and "Building Blocks" which provide an overview to grammar and sentence structure concepts.

Functions in Sentences

The chart below indicates functions that the building blocks, or sentence parts, play in a sentence.

subject	a person, place, thing, or idea that names "who" or "what" a sentence is about
verb (predicate)	the action of a sentence or word that links the subject to a descriptor
object: direct	a word or words that receive the action of a sentence
objects: indirect	a noun or pronoun that tells to or for whom the action is done
modifier	a word or phrase that describes or limits another word or group of words
complement	a word or group of words that renames or describes a subject
link	words that link one part of a sentence to another

These building blocks are made up of parts of speech, each with a specific job or function.

Parts of a Sentence: A Quick Review

Showing the most basic building blocks of a sentence, the following chart shows the eight parts of speech, as well as the specific function(s) that each part of speech performs in sentences. Each of these parts of speech will be covered later in this chapter.

Part of Speech	Definition and Function
noun	naming a person, place, thing, or idea, a word that can function in a sentence as a subject, object, or complement
pronoun	substituting for a noun, a noun phrase, or another pronoun, a word that can function as a subject, object, or complement
verb	a word that shows an action or state of being

Part of Speech	Definition and Function
preposition	a word that links a noun or pronoun and related modifier to another word to show relationships such as time and space
conjunction	a word that links one word or word group to a similar word or word group
adjective (and articles)	a word or group of words that modifies, limits, or describes a noun or pronoun
adverb	a word that modifies or provides information about a verb, adverb, or adjective
interjection	standing alone, a word or words used to express emotion

By placing these sentence building blocks in specific combinations or patterns, the larger parts of a sentence—the subject, verbs, phrases, and clauses—work together and support each other to build a complete sentence. These larger parts of sentences have specific functions in a sentence just as single words have specific functions in a sentence. The following chart shows all the various parts or sentence building blocks and the functions they play.

Building Blocks/Part of a Sentence	Functions as
subject (or noun phrase as subject)	the "who" or "what" that performs the action ▶ *Jack* reads the newspaper every morning. the "who" or "what" that is being described or renamed ▶ *Jack* is a well-known stockbroker. the "who" or "what" that is receiving the action ▶ The *newspaper* is read by Jack every morning.
verb (or verb phrase)	the action or linking verb of the sentence ▶ Jack *reads* the newspaper every morning.

Building Blocks/Part of a Sentence	Functions as
phrase: prepositional	an adverb or adjective modifier ▶ Jack reads the newspaper *at the breakfast table.*
phrase: gerund	noun in the role of subject, subject complement, direct object, or object of the preposition ▶ Jack likes *reading the newspaper* every morning.
phrase: participial	an adjective ▶ *Sitting at the breakfast table,* Jack reads the newspaper.
phrase: infinitive	a noun in the role of subject, direct object, or subject complement; modifier in the role of adjective or adverb. ▶ Jack likes *to read the newspaper* every morning.
phrase: appositive	the renaming of another noun ▶ Jack, *a Wall Street broker,* likes to read the newspaper.
clause: main clause (must contain at least one subject and one verb)	a complete thought in a sentence ▶ *Jack reads the newspaper every morning*
clause: adverb clause (contains a subject and verb but dependent on main clause to complete the meaning)	a modifier of verbs, adjectives, or other adverbs; answers questions: When? Where? Why? How? Under what conditions? To what degree? ▶ *When he drinks his morning coffee,* Jack reads the newspaper.
clause: adjective clause (contains a subject and verb but dependent on main clause to complete the meaning)	a modifier of nouns or pronouns and answers questions: Which one? What kind of? ▶ Jack, *who is a Wall Street broker,* likes to read the newspaper every morning.

Building Blocks/Part of a Sentence	Functions as
clause: noun clause (dependent on main clause)	subject, object, object of a preposition, subject complement ▶ Jack likes to read the newspaper which reports about *that which is taking place on the stock market.*

A sentence can be built by continually adding the other parts of speech or parts of a sentence to the most basic unit: the subject and verb. A student can build a sentence from all the different types of building blocks by starting with a **subject** and **verb** unit.

▶ <u>Chelsea and Sue</u> <u>are reading</u>.

A student can then add

- objects: indirect and direct
- other parts of speech: a pronoun, preposition, conjunction, adjective, and adverb
- clauses: main, adverb, adjective, and noun clauses
- phrases: gerund, participial, infinitive, and appositive

By using all the possible parts of speech and other sentence building blocks, students can create sentences that include pertinent details.

   participial   phrase   *adj clause*
▶ Sitting on small chairs, <u>Chelsea and Sue</u>, who are both college students, <u>are</u>

  adv   *IO   appositive phrase   DO   prep phrase*
quietly <u>reading</u> to the little girl, a fidgety six-year-old, a book in the library,

conj   *main clause*   *adverb clause*   *noun clause*
but the girl isn't listening because she is distracted by that which is taking

          adj   *infinitive phrase*   *main cl* *gerund phrase*
place at the next table; to get her attention, they stop reading the book.

The above example might be too long for an essay, but the example demonstrates that using the building blocks available in the English language will help students develop more complete and complex ideas in a sentence. When you have finished reading and working through this chapter as well as Chapter Four (subjects and verbs) and Chapter Five (phrases, clauses and sentences), you should have a good understanding of the functioning of all sentence parts. You should also be able to help students put complete thoughts together in more complex ways and help them use all the parts of speech and parts of sentences in ways that are grammatically correct.

Parts of Speech

To accomplish the task of writing grammatically correct sentences that convey complete and well-developed thoughts, students must be able to identify nouns and pronouns, then verbs, and then identify prepositions and prepositional phrases. It is important that students not confuse the object of the preposition with the subject of a sentence since nouns and pronouns function as both subject and objects. While subjects of sentences will be discussed in the next chapter, parts of speech will be presented in this chapter in this order:

nouns	adjectives
pronouns	adverbs
verbs	conjunctions
prepositions	interjections

Nouns

A **noun** names a **person, place, thing**, or **idea**. Nouns can be common nouns (*goat, tree, house*) or proper nouns (*Abraham Lincoln*, the *Golden Gate Bridge*). Proper nouns are capitalized.

Person	man, firefighter, officer, President Washington
Place	city, park, mall, Seattle, Disneyland
Thing	car, thoughts, pen, house, record, Washington Monument
Idea	wisdom, altruism, sincerity, faith, love, hope, Judaism

Pronouns

Pronouns take the place of common or proper nouns. Below are examples of pronouns listed by type.

Personal	I, we, he, she, it, they
Possessive	my, his, her, their
Demonstrative	this, these, those
Indefinite	anybody, someone, everybody
Reflexive	myself, himself, herself, ourselves, themselves
Interrogative	in questions: who, which, what
Relative	who, whom, whose, which, that

The personal pronouns are classified by person, number (plural or singular), and case. The subjective case pronouns are used when the pronoun functions as a subject. The objective case pronouns are used when the pronoun functions as an object.

▶ *We* saw a movie today.   [pronoun as subject]
▶ Harriet gave *him* a present.   [pronoun as object]

The following chart lists the pronouns by case and person showing the singular and plural forms.

Person	Subjective Case		Objective Case		Possessive Case	
	Singular	*Plural*	*Singular*	*Plural*	*Singular*	*Plural*
First	I	we	me	us	my, mine	our, ours
Second	you	you	you	you	your, yours	your, yours
Third	he, she, it	they	him, her, it	them	his, her, hers, its	their, theirs
Relative	who	who	whom	whom	whose	whose

Verbs

Verbs are either action verbs that describe the action of the sentence or are linking verbs (state of being verbs) that link a noun, pronoun, or adjective to the subject.

Action verbs	walk, write, run, watch, jump, decide, think, exist
Linking verbs	is, am, are, was, were, be, being, been, seem, appear, become

A **main verb** denotes the main action or main state of being in a sentence. It is derived from the basic verb form without the auxiliary or helping verb. Verbs show tense in the present, past, or participial verb form. Many verbs form the past participle by adding –*ed* or –*en* to the base verb. However, some verbs do not follow this pattern, so they are known as **irregular verbs** because they do not use –*ed* or –*en* to form the past participle. Most grammar books contain a list of irregular verbs. The following chart shows a brief explanation of verb forms.

Present: changes for singular and plural form	Past: uses -ed form or past tense irregular form	Present Participial: uses a helping verb plus –ing form or irregular form	Past Participle uses the –ed form of the verb or the form that normally uses the helping verbs has, have, had
jump, jumps	jumped	jumping	jumped
teach, teaches	taught	teaching	taught
sing	sang	singing	sung
am, is, are	was, were	being	been

Helping verbs, also known as **auxiliary verbs**, indicate time and tense for both the action and linking verb. The helping or auxiliary verbs are forms of *have*, *do*, and *be* as well as the modals *may, must, might, should, would, could, shall, will*, and *can*.

> ▶ Fredrique *is debating* against the first place team.
> [The helping verb *is* and the main verb *debating* show an action in progress.]
> ▶ Fredrique *might debate* in the tournament next week.
> [The modal *might* and the main verb *debate* show an action that is possible.]

Complete verbs contain at least a main verb plus any helping or auxiliary verbs. The term *predicate* is used by some instructors to refer to the complete verb. Verb tenses and verbs working together with subjects will be discussed in Chapter Four along with grammatical terms associated with verbs.

Practice 1. Identifying Nouns, Pronouns, Main Verbs, and Auxiliary (Helping) Verbs

In the following sentences, write **N** above all nouns, **Pro** above all pronouns, **MV** above all main verbs, and **Aux** above all auxiliary (helping) verbs. You may check your answers in the answer key at the end of the book.

> *Pro Aux   MV   N*
> ▶ He was peddling arduously during the bike race.

1. Lance Armstrong has written his autobiography about the Tour de France and his battle with cancer.
2. Some people see Armstrong as a hero.
3. Like Lance Armstrong, the ice skater Scott Hamilton has overcome cancer and continues to participate in his sport.

4. They have demonstrated the strength of willpower in overcoming adversity.

5. Armstrong has been speaking regularly to groups about cancer survival.

Prepositions

Prepositions are connecting words that show place, time, direction, or condition; their function in a sentence is to connect a noun, pronoun, gerund, phrase, or noun clause with another word. As a result, prepositions never appear in a sentence alone. Instead, they appear in a phrase (a group of words) that begins with a preposition and ends with a noun or pronoun (or gerund phrase or noun clause). This phrase is called a prepositional phrase, and this entire phrase functions as an adjective or adverb. Below are some of the most common single word prepositions that introduce prepositional phrases.

aboard	below	into	through
about	beneath	like	throughout
above	beside(s)	near	till
across	between	of	to
after	beyond	off	toward(s)
against	by	on	under
along	concerning	onto	underneath
amid	considering	outside	until
among	down	over	unto
around	during	past	up
as	for	per	upon
at	from	regarding	via
before	in	respecting	with
behind	inside	round	within
		since	without

Some prepositions consist of two or more words and are called phrasal prepositions:

according to	because of	in spite of
ahead of	contrary to	in view of
apart from	due to	on account of
as far as	in place of	owing to

A preposition introduces a prepositional phrase: *in the house, on the road, in front of a truck, to her, by fleeing the scene, to whom it may concern*. A preposition is always followed by a noun or pronoun, gerund phrase, or noun clause that is called the **object of the preposition**. In the above examples, the words *house, road, front, truck,* and *her* as well as the phrase, *fleeing the scene* and the clause *whom it may concern* are the objects of the prepositions.

Some prepositions appear after a verb and form a two-word verb such as *look up* or *put down*. These prepositions are being used as **particles**, and, in this case, the preposition becomes part of the verb to create a **phrasal verb** or **prepositional verb**. Some prepositions, when used as a particle, can be separated from the verb while others, called **bound prepositions**, must be used immediately after the verb for the preposition to have meaning.

▶ The car *broke down* on the freeway.   *but not*
▶ The car *broke* on the freeway *down*.

Because the words *broke down* are bound together to give the verb meaning, the preposition *down* cannot be separated from the verb *broke*. However, depending on the meaning of the verb, some particles may be split:

▶ You need to *back up* your file.   *or*
▶ You need to *back* your file *up*.

Chapter Eight also contains information about bound prepositions in reference to ESL writers.

Helping students: In assignments, students may have to find subjects and verbs in sentences. When helping them with such an assignment, remind students that subjects or verbs are never found within prepositional phrases. Because students often confuse the object of the preposition with the sentence's subject, they should identify all prepositional phrases before they identify subjects and verbs.

Practice 2 Identifying Prepositions and Prepositional Phrases

In the sentences below, identify each **preposition** by writing **prep** above the word and placing parentheses around each complete **prepositional phrase**. You may check your answers in the answer key at the end of the book.

                 prep   *prep*   *prep*
▶ An old chair rotting (with age) sat (on the front porch) (of the vacant

   prep   *prep*
house) (with a "no-trespassing" sign) (on the front door).

1. During the Depression, people tried to earn money by selling an apple for five cents.
2. On New Year's Eve in 1928, Americans were spending money without a care, but by New Year's Eve 1929, many Americans no longer felt the joy of celebrating.

3. In the Dust Bowl years, families packed suitcases with all their necessary items, threw their few possessions in the car, and took off for California.
4. For a long time, people avoided saving money in a bank because of the many bank failures after the Stock Market Crash of 1929.
5. However, today my parents have instilled in me the value of saving money in a bank account.

Adjectives / Adverbs

Adjectives and **adverbs** are different parts of speech, yet they function similarly in sentences—they both are modifiers. Though various forms of words, phrases, and clauses function as modifiers, in their simplest form there are only two kinds of modifiers—adjectives and adverbs. The function of a modifier, whether adjective or adverb, is to describe, change, limit, or alter the meaning of another word.

Adjectives modify only nouns or pronouns.

▶ The *flower* vendor sold *red* roses, *white* carnations, and *purple* delphiniums.
▶ Charles Lindbergh made the *first solo nonstop transatlantic* flight in 1927.

The articles *a, an*, and *the* are always adjectives because they mark a noun. Articles will be discussed more in Chapter Eight.

Adverbs modify verbs, adjectives, and adverbs. Students can identify an adverb because adverbs answer the questions *When? Where? Why? How? Under what conditions?* or *To what degree?* Many adverbs are easily identified because they end in *ly*. However, the following words, which do not end in *ly*, also function as adverbs: *always, also, already, here, never, not, now, often, quite, seldom, soon, still, then, there, too, very, well.*

▶ Soaring *gracefully*, the airplane rose into the San Diego sky.
▶ People *still* marvel that Lindbergh made such a flight in 1927.

Helping students: To determine if a modifier is an adjective or an adverb, identify the word being modified. If the word being modified is a noun or pronoun, the modifier is an adjective. The modifier is an adverb, if the word being modified is a verb, adjective, or adverb.

Practice 3 *Identifying Adjective and Adverbs*

In each sentence, underline the adjectives (other than articles) and adverbs and mark each one as **adj** or **adv**. Then draw an arrow to the word that the adjective or adverb modifies. You may check your answers in the answer key at the end of the book.

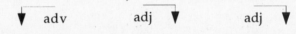

▶ The road wound <u>deeply</u> into the <u>dark</u> woods where <u>dense</u> trees

adj ▼

sheltered the <u>brilliant</u> sunlight.

1. Hurriedly, the frantic teacher ran to the copy center to run off the final exam that she had inconveniently misplaced.
2. Yesterday, Dan and Emma saw the video version of the thriller, *The Sum of All Fears*.
3. Though many people think swashbuckling movies help contribute to the mystic of the sport of fencing, for the skilled fencer, the appealing challenge includes the intellectual strategy, the athletic endurance, and the graceful movement.
4. A fencing bout lasts only ten minutes, yet the sport of fencing is extremely exhausting.
5. Never in all of the years performing Shakespearean plays, had the actors seen an audience who was quite so exuberant.

Conjunctions

Conjunction literally means *to join with*. Conjunctions join parts of sentences, complete sentences, or even paragraphs. The various kinds of conjunctions include

coordinating, subordinating, conjunctive adverb, and **correlative**

1. **Coordinating conjunctions** are used to show specific relationships between equal parts in a sentence. For instance, coordinating conjunctions can join two or more nouns, two or more verbs, or two or more prepositional phrases. They cannot join a noun with a verb. Each coordinating conjunction indicates a specific relationship of the words joined. The table below lists the coordinating conjunctions and the relationship that the coordinating conjunction has with words, phrases, and clauses.

Relationship	Coordinating Conjunction
Addition	and
Contrast	but, yet
Cause or result	so, for
Alternatives	or, nor

Students can easily remember the list of coordinating conjunctions by remembering the acronym **FANBOYS** or **BOYSFAN**.

The acronym **BOYSFAN** stands for <u>b</u>ut, <u>o</u>r, <u>y</u>et, <u>s</u>o, <u>f</u>or, <u>a</u>nd, <u>n</u>or.

2. **Subordinating conjunctions** introduce subordinating clauses, also called adverb clauses, that are dependent on main clauses to complete their meaning; thus, **subordinate clauses** are often called **dependent clauses**. A subordinating conjunction alerts the reader to the relationship between the idea expressed in the main clause and the idea expressed in the dependent clause.

Relationship	Subordinating Conjunctions
Time	after, as soon as, before, once, until, when, whenever, while
Place	where, wherever
Cause	as, because, since
Condition	even if, if, unless
Contrast	although, even though, though, whereas, while
Comparison	than, as, as if, as though
Purpose	so that, that

▶ *Before* the play started, everyone waited for the doors to open.
▶ The audience gave the actors an ovation *when* the play ended.

3. **Conjunctive adverbs**, often referred to as transitional words or expressions, provide a transition from one thought to another in a sentence or between sentences and paragraphs to show the relationship between thoughts. Writers can use conjunctive adverbs to show specific relationships between ideas as shown in the list and examples below:

To add a related idea: *also, furthermore, in addition, in fact, moreover, next*

▶ Franz Liszt composed symphonies and conducted operas and concerts; *in addition*, he taught piano and composition.

To illustrate: *as an illustration, for example, for instance, specifically, such as*

▶ People like to vacation in many beautiful spots *such as* Hawaii, Tahiti, Paris, London, and New York City.

To show cause and effect: *as a result, consequently, hence, therefore, thus*

▶ I studied for the final until 1:30 in the morning; *as a result*, I had a hard time getting up.

To conclude or summarize: *in conclusion, in other words, in summary, therefore, to conclude, to summarize*

▶ *In conclusion*, the world needs to look at creating solutions to avoid destruction of sensitive regions of the earth.

To contrast: *conversely, however, in contrast, in fact, instead, nevertheless, nonetheless, on the contrary, on the other hand, otherwise*

▶ Many Americans consider George Washington to be a Revolutionary War hero; *in fact*, he is also a hero because he was the first president of the United States.

To compare: *also, analogously, analogous to, compared to, in comparison with, in the same manner, likewise, similarly, similar to*

▶ A hurricane can be an intense and devastating storm; *likewise*, a typhoon or cyclone can produce tremendous devastation.

To indicate sequence: *first, second, third, next, finally, then*

▶ I have many tasks to finish. *First*, I have to set up a spreadsheet and *next* enter the data; *finally*, I will analyze the figures.

4. **Correlative Conjunctions** are paired words that must be used in parallel structure in a sentence: *either . . . or, neither . . . nor, not only . . . but also, whether . . . or*

▶ *Neither* the weather bureau *nor* the local radio warned the public about the rapidly rising storm.

Practice 4 Identifying Conjunctions

Underline and identify each conjunction as coordinating, subordinating, conjunctive adverb, or correlative. Write **coord**, **sub**, **conj adv**, or **corr**.

                    coord   *conj adv*
▶ The train was late, <u>so</u> Carlos couldn't leave town on time; <u>consequently</u>, he was upset.

1. Vegans will neither eat meat nor consume dairy products.

2. Some employment applications have been filled out completely and neatly; therefore, the applicants are more likely to be looked at favorably.
3. These journal articles look interesting and supply informative data.
4. Although writing an essay is a process, students and other writers have found that people do not use the same methods to initially organize their thoughts.
5. After students receive assignments, they can use many prewriting methods that generate ideas and thoughts about their topic.
6. Brainstorming, clustering, listing, or freewriting are all good methods of generating ideas; however, some students just sit down and start writing.
7. Students should develop a thesis statement because every essay should have a central point.
8. Students can generate either a scratch outline or formal outline which lists points and support.
9. Organizing an essay well is important, yet using good sentence structure adds to an essay's readability.
10. Because students, who are enrolled in classes requiring essays, can find extra help in a writing center, these centers are usually busy.

Interjections

Although used infrequently in essays or academic writing, an **interjection** is a word (or words) standing alone in a sentence that interjects emotion. An interjection is usually followed by an exclamation mark.

▶ *Hey!*
▶ *Oh, my!*
▶ *Wow!* I got an A on the last test.

Chapter 4

Sentence Building Blocks: Subjects, Verbs, and Pronouns Working Together

Along with knowing the names of the first type of building blocks, which are the eight parts of speech, students also need to know how to arrange these building blocks in meaningful patterns to construct a sentence. These blocks are arranged according to how each part functions in a sentence and works together with other parts. In this chapter, you will look at

- the subject of a sentence
- the verb: both an action verb and linking verb
- subject–verb agreement
- pronoun agreement

Subjects

The **subject** of a sentence is the "who" or "what" the sentence is about. That is, a subject is the person, place, thing, idea, or concept that answers the question "who" or "what" in reference to the verb. The subject can be one word, two or more words (called a compound subject), a phrase, or even a clause.

Helping students: When discussing the subject of a sentence, suggest that students first find the verb and then any prepositional phrases before they identify the subject.

> *subj verb   prep phrase*
> ▶ John runs (around the track daily).

As you help students analyze the above sentence, you might do the following:

- Ask them to identify the word that describes the action; the action in this sentence is the word *runs*, the verb. However, if the sentence includes a state of being verb or linking verb, students may have to look for a verb that is a form of *to be*.
- Suggest that they underline the subject with one line and the verb with two lines.
- Ask them to look for any prepositional phrases.
- Use a table that lists prepositions to help students identify prepositions.
- Have students place parentheses around prepositional phrases.
- Have students identify the object of the preposition.
- Explain to students that they will never find the subject in a prepositional phrase.
- Help students determine the subject of the sentence.
- To find the subject of a sentence, ask them, "Who or what *runs*?" For the above example sentence, the answer is *John*, so *John* is the subject of the sentence.
- Remind students that they may need to look for more than one subject or one verb. The subject of a sentence may be a compound subject: two subjects joined by *and* or *or*. Also, the sentence may contain a compound verb: two verbs joined by *and* or *or*.

▶ Juan and Ramon lift weights daily.   [compound subject]
▶ Juan works out and lifts weights daily.   [compound verb]

Verbs and Verbals

Verbs are either action verbs that describe the action of the sentence or are linking verbs (state of being verbs) that link a noun, pronoun, or adjective to the subject. Verbs in their various forms show **tense** and indicate the **time** when the action takes place. They may also show **person** and **number**. A verb can show **active** or **passive** voice as well as indicate **indicative, imperative,** or **subjunctive mood.**

Tense. Verbs change tense to indicate the time frame in which the action takes place. A tense may tell the reader that the action takes place in the present, past, or future.

Present   The office assistant sorts the mail everyday.
Past   The office assistant sorted the mail yesterday.
Future   The office assistant will sort the mail tomorrow.

The present, past, and future tenses are called the simple tenses because they express a simple time frame. Other tenses express aspects of present, past, and future. They show a more complex time, and in some cases, a time that is dependent on another action taking place. Below are the simple, progressive, perfect, and perfect progressive, the aspects of the three tenses.

Simple present tense is used to indicate action taking place currently or regularly; **simple past tense** is used to indicate an action already completed; and **simple future tense** is used to indicate an action that will occur in the future.

Simple present	I jog, he jogs, they jog
Simple past	I jogged, he jogged, they jogged
Simple future	I will jog, he will jog, they will jog

Perfect tenses are used to indicate an action that began in the past and is linked to another action; the action takes place (**present perfect**), took place (**past perfect**), or will take place (**future perfect**) at the time of another action. The presence of the helping verb *have, has,* or *had* indicates that a verb is in a perfect tense.

Present perfect	I have jogged, he has jogged, they have jogged
Past perfect	I had jogged, he had jogged, they had jogged
Future perfect	I will have jogged, he/they will have jogged

Progressive tenses describe actions that are in progress either presently, in the past, or will be ongoing in the future. The progressive verb tenses use a form of the verb *be* as a helping verb plus the *–ing* form of a verb.

Present progressive	I am jogging, he is jogging, they are jogging
Past progressive	I was jogging, he was jogging, they were jogging
Future progressive	I will be jogging, he will be jogging, they will be jogging

Perfect progressive tense is used when the length of time that an action has been in progress is indicated. In the perfect progressive tense, two helping verbs are needed: a form of *have* (*has/have/had*) plus the helping verb *been*.

Present perfect progressive	I/he/she/they have/has been jogging
Past perfect progressive	I/he/she/they had been jogging
Future perfect progressive	I/he/she/they will have been jogging

Usually native speakers naturally express themselves with the correct verb tense while non-native English speakers spend years learning these tenses. Many ESL students who take basic writing classes are learning how to use tenses correctly. When working with ESL students, you may have to focus on verb tenses, especially the form as well as shifts. Chapter Eight will discuss additional information about verbs as relating to ESL students.

Helping students: As you work with students on verbs and help them learn the concepts of time and aspect, you may face specific questions about verb tenses. To help students further, you might

- Work with them on examples in a grammar book.
- Offer them verb tense handouts.
- Suggest that they work through verb tense modules of a grammar software program.

Other Terms Associated with Verbs

As students learn basic grammar terms, some may be frustrated by verbs. Listed below are other specific terms associated with verbs that may be problematic for students.

Irregular verbs. Many verbs form the past tense by adding an *–ed*, and they form the past participle by using the *–ed* form of the verb. However, not all verbs form the past tense and past participle this simply. Some verbs change forms in different manners and are known as irregular verbs. *Teach* and *choose* are examples of irregular verbs in the past and participle verb forms. For the verb *teach*, the past tense is not *teached*; the past tense and past participle are *taught* while for the verb *choose*, the past tense is *chose* and the past participle is *chosen*.

Helping students: Students must either memorize the irregular forms or consult a verb form chart. When students wish to determine an irregular verb form, be sure to direct students to standard grammar books that usually have charts or lists of irregular verbs. Another useful resource is the dictionary where the verb tenses are listed as part of the definition entry. For visual learners, looking at an irregular verb chart may be one way to help them remember irregular verb tense formation and to help them memorize these exceptions. For auditory learners, be sure to repeat the forms of the verbs aloud to them several times.

Transitive and intransitive verbs. Verbs can be classified as **transitive** or **intransitive** verbs depending on the presence of an object.

A **transitive verb** always has a direct object that receives the action of the verb. Transitive verbs need the direct object to be present in the sentence for the sentence to have meaning. The normal sentence pattern with this type of verb is subject – verb – object.

▶ The <u>boy hit</u> the *ball*.

The verb *hit* is a transitive verb because the object, *ball*, is receiving the action of the verb.

Helping students: To find a direct object in the subject – verb – object sentence pattern, after the verb ask *"Who?"* or *"What?"* The boy hit *what?* The answer is *ball*, so *ball* is the direct object.

An intransitive verb does not have an object, so the normal sentence pattern for this type of verb is subject – verb.

▶ Stephen awakens slowly.

Awakens is an intransitive verb because the action of *awakens* is complete in itself; the sentence requires no object to complete its meaning.

Linking verbs. This type of verb links the subject of the sentence to words that complement, describe the subject, or rename the subject; several of the most commonly used linking verbs are the *to be* verbs (*is, am, are, was, were*), as well as verbs such as *appear, become,* and *seem.* Sentences with linking verbs do not take objects, so linking verbs are intransitive verbs. The normal linking verb sentence pattern is **subject – linking verb – subject complement**.

▶ The Seneca Falls Convention was the *first convention devoted to the women's right movement.*

Helping students: To identify a linking verb, think of the linking verb as an equal (=) sign. Linking verbs rename or describe the subject, and the word(s) that come after the linking verb are known as the subject complement, which can be a noun or noun phrase, pronoun, or adjective.

▶ The girl is (=) a *hero.*   [noun]
▶ The boy is (=) *he.*   [pronoun]
▶ The man appears (=) *happy.*   [adjective]

A linking verb is often referred to as a state of being verb or a stative verb.

▶ Erin *is* happy. [Erin's state of being is happy.]

Verbals. Derived from verbs but not functioning as verbs in a sentence, verbals can be used like nouns, adverbs, or adjectives. They can function as subjects, objects, or modifiers. Often students write essays with fragmented sentences because they are using verbals instead of a correct verb that shows time and aspect. Verbals take three forms that are known as **participles**, **gerunds**, or **infinitives**.

1. A **participle** modifies a noun, so it functions as an adjective. A present participle is the *–ing* form of a verb, and the past participle is the *–ed* form, the form of the verb that requires *have, has,* or *had*.

▶ The *working* mother dropped off her toddler at day care. [present participle]
▶ The *excited* girl went out to play. [past participle]

A participle used as a verbal does not have a helping verb. Notice that with the helping verb, a participle shows action. However, without the helping verb, the participle functions as an adjective.

▶ The government forces *have defeated* the rebels.   [action]
▶ The *defeated* rebels retreated.   [adjective]

2. A **gerund** is the *–ing* verb form that functions as a noun but does not use a helping verb.

▶ My daughter loves *baking* fancy desserts.

3. An **infinitive** is formed with *to* plus the base form of a verb. An infinitive can never function as the main verb in a sentence; instead, it functions as a noun, adjective, or adverb.

▶ He wanted *to sail* in his boat, but the lake was choppy.

Finite and nonfinite verbs. Some instructors may use the terms *finite* and *nonfinite* to describe verbs and verbals.

Finite verbs are finished verbs; they show the action or state of being.

▶ The executives *decided* on a plan for raising profits next year.
▶ Many children *watch* television too much and *exercise* too little.
▶ Mark *seems* sad today.

Nonfinite verbs are verbals—participles, gerunds, or infinitives. Verbals do not show tense, nor are they finished.

▶ *Studying* for finals exhausts most college students.

Practice 5 Identifying Verbs and Verbals

Underline the **verbs** and **verbals** in the following sentences. Above each verb write the tense and aspect (i.e. present perfect) and above each **verbal** write the type of verbal: participle, gerund, or infinitive.

 past prog   *infinitive*
▶ The little boy <u>was crying</u> because he had <u>to go</u> to the hospital for a test.

1.   Ignored by the owner, the dogs chewed on the furniture.
2.   Is that football player succeeding at kicking field goals?
3.   Sprinting down the street, the police officer caught up with the suspect.
4.   The teacher wants the class to be on time for the test.
5.   Please work in the laboratory to find the virus causing the epidemic.
6.   The blazing fire has been warming the room nicely.
7.   Working every night after his regular job, Todd will finish the bathroom remodel in six weeks.
8.   Had Tim and Debbie been hunting with bows and arrows?
9.   The hot weather had caused everyone to seek shelter at the indoor ice rink.
10. Riding the evening train home helps him to relax after work.

Voice: active and passive. In developing writing skills, students should use active voice because active voice verbs add zest to the writing, are lively and interesting, and express thoughts effectively. English sentences depend on verbs to breathe life into nouns for dynamic and interesting sentences. When students use active voice, their sentences will be strong and to the point.

> **Active voice** is formed when the subject of the sentence is the "doer" of the action.

▶ The speeding <u>car hit</u> the lamppost.
▶ <u>She</u> <u>drove</u> the car into the garage.

In the first example, the subject *car* performs or is the doer of the action *hit*. In the second sentence, the verb or action is *drove*, and the subject *she* performs or is the doer of the action.

> **Passive voice** is created by using a form of the helping (auxiliary) verb *to be* with a main verb in the past participle form (the form ending in –*ed* used with *have*, *has*, or *had*). In passive voice, the subject receives the action. Only transitive verbs can be passive.

▶ The <u>lamppost was hit</u> by a speeding car.
▶ The <u>car was driven</u> into the garage.

In the first passive voice example, the subject *lamppost* receives the action, and the real doer of the action is buried in the prepositional phrase. In the second passive voice example, the actual driver of the car is absent from the sentence altogether. Who drove the car? The emphasis in the second sentence is on the car, not on any performer or doer of the action.

Helping students: Passive voice has a place in writing, especially in science writing when an experiment's results can be more important than who performed the experiment. However, in college composition, students should use passive voice rarely. Passive voice creates an impersonal or distant tone, and overuse or inappropriate use in essay writing leads to weak and boring sentences. When working with students, suggest that they change passive voice sentences to active voice sentences. They can often rewrite a passive voice sentence by making the object of the preposition the subject of the sentence. At other times, especially when the intended performer is absent, the rewrite is not as simple. In this case, you will need to help students discover the noun that is the actual performer and make that noun the subject.

▶ To get exercise, her <u>dog is let out</u> everyday at sunset.

Who or what let the dog out? Students may have to make several attempts at rewriting to eliminate the passive voice, but students will produce more strongly worded sentences and have more clarity when they rewrite and use active voice.

> *First Revision*: To get exercise, Alicia lets her dog out everyday at sunset.
> *Second Revision*: Alicia lets her dog out for exercise everyday at sunset.

Practice 6 Passive Voice Versus Active Voice

Rewrite the following sentences to eliminate the passive voice. In some instances, you may have to add a "doer" of the action to use active voice.

▶ A new vaccine was discovered for the virulent disease.
   Repair: The pharmaceutical researcher discovered a new vaccine for the virulent disease.

1. Was the car repaired by the dealership?
2. The house was constructed in only five months.
3. The earth's environment has been polluted.
4. An around-the-world trip was enjoyed by Samantha during the summer.
5. During winter break, Math 90 was taken in only three weeks by many students.

Mood. There are three moods or three verb forms that show a writer's attitude.

In the **indicative mood**, the writer is stating fact or opinion.

▶ Leonardo da Vinci sketched a prototype of an experimental flying machine.

In the **imperative mood**, the writer is giving commands or directions. This mood is used in how-to or process analysis essays that break down a procedure into steps. Often a sentence in the imperative mood has an unstated subject, the implied *you*.

> ▶ First, put the pot on to boil. Next, add oil to the water. Finally, add the pasta to the boiling water.
> [*You* is the implied subject in each of the sentences showing how to cook pasta.]

In the **subjunctive mood**, the writer is expressing either a condition, a wish, or a request, demand, or recommendation.

To express a **condition contrary to fact**, the writer creates a subordinate clause beginning with the subordinate conjunctions *if* or *unless* (and sometimes *when*).

> ▶ *If* Sean *were* going home, I *would* go with him.
> ▶ *If* they *had been* on time, they *would have seen* the performance.

To express a **wish**, use the simple past tense verb or the past tense *were*. To form a wish about the past, use *had* as the helping verb plus the past participle. Sometimes, but not always, the dependent clause begins with *that*.

> ▶ I *wish* I *were* six feet tall.   [I wish *that* I were six feet tall.]

To make a **request**, a **demand**, or **recommendation**, the writer will use certain verbs such as *ask, insist, recommend, request, suggest, demand, propose,* or *urge* in the main clause and use the base form of the verb (regardless of person and number of the subject) in the dependent clause.

> ▶ Andrea's obstetrician *suggested that* she *take* vitamins during the next nine months.
> [The verb in the *that* clause is the base form *take* and not the third person singular *takes*.]

Practice 7 Identifying Subjects, Verbs, and Prepositional Phrases

In the following sentences, identify the **subject(s)** with a single underline, the **complete verb** with a double underline, and place parentheses around **prepositional phrases**.

> ▶ (After the board meeting,) the <u>executives</u> <u>were continuing</u> to talk about the problem.

1. Did the thunder and lightning scare all the youngsters at camp during the night?
2. Finish the project before you leave.

3. Most colleges have fewer students in attendance during the summer.
4. The pond was frozen and had become slippery during the big ice storm.
5. Across the horizon, the hikers saw the summit that they still needed to cross.

Agreement

There are two types of agreement: subject–verb agreement and pronoun agreement.

Subject-Verb Agreement

Subjects and verbs work together in a sentence, so they must agree in number. If a subject is singular, the verb needs to be the singular verb form. If the subject is plural, the verb needs to be the plural verb form. This working together is called subject–verb agreement.

THE BASIC RULE OF SUBJECT–VERB AGREEMENT

1. A singular subject takes a singular verb form while plural subjects take plural verb forms. Subjects joined by *and* (called a compound subject) also take plural verbs.

   ▶ The new closing <u>pitcher</u> consistently <u>throws</u> strikes.
   [Singular subject takes a singular verb form.]
   ▶ <u>Batters</u> <u>feel</u> frustrated when <u>pitchers</u> <u>throw</u> no-hit games.
   [Plural subjects take plural verb forms.]
   ▶ The <u>pitcher</u> and the <u>catcher</u> <u>congratulate</u> each other as they walk to the dugout.
   [Compound subject takes a plural verb form.]

Helping students: When students have difficulty with subject–verb agreement, discuss the letter –s. Ann Raimes in *Keys for Writers* suggests the "one –s rule."[1] Her rule reminds students that the subject and verb both cannot end in an –s. Either the subject is plural by adding an –s, or the verb form is the third person singular by adding an –s. Remind students that adding an –s to a noun creates the plural noun (one *tree* but two *trees*) while adding an –s to a present tense verb creates the singular, third person verb: *he walks, she walks, it walks.* If students are confused, have them substitute *he, she,* or *it* for a singular subject and *they* for a plural subject. Then, they can analyze the sentence for correct subject–verb agreement.

OTHER SUBJECT–VERB AGREEMENT RULES OR PRINCIPLES

2. Intervening words may be confused with the subject of the sentence. The verb must agree with only its subject.

   ▶ His <u>toolbox</u> of antique tools <u>appears</u> to be one hundred years old.
   [*Toolbox* is the subject, not *tools*, which is the object of the preposition.]

3. Most indefinite pronouns (*each, either, neither one, no one, everyone, everybody, anyone, anybody, someone, somebody*) take a singular verb.

   ▶ <u>Each</u> of the students <u>brings</u> his or her own lunch.
   ▶ <u>Somebody has broken</u> the window.

4. The indefinite pronouns *both, few, many, several* take the plural verb form.

   ▶ <u>Several</u> of the teachers <u>attend</u> the workshop every month.

5. The indefinite pronouns *all, any, half, most, more, none,* and *some* require an examination of the intervening prepositional phrase. If the object of the prepositional phrase is singular, the verb form should be singular. If the object of the prepositional phrase is plural, then the verb form is plural.

   ▶ <u>Half</u> of the melons <u>look</u> rotten.
   [Since *melons* is plural, *half* is plural, so the correct verb is *look*.]
   ▶ <u>All</u> of the fruit <u>looks</u> rotten.
   [Since *fruit* is a collective noun, *all* is singular, so the correct verb is *looks*.]

6. With *either . . . or* or *neither . . . nor*, the verb should agree with the subject closest to the verb.

   ▶ Neither the picketers nor management <u>wants</u> to end the strike.
   ▶ Neither management nor the picketers <u>want</u> to end the strike.

7. Collective nouns such as *team, committee, group, family, class, mob,* and *government* commonly use a singular verb form.

   ▶ <u>Government borrows</u> money thereby increasing the national debt.

8. Expressions of time, money, measurement, and fractions use a singular verb form when the amount is regarded as one unit.

▶ A million <u>dollars</u> <u>is</u> enough money to fund the new project.

9. Titles such as organizations or books that end in –s use the singular verb form.

▶ The <u>Veterans of Foreign Wars</u> <u>contributes</u> to American patriotism.

10. Some nouns, such as economics, robotics, or physics, end in –s and use the singular verb form. The word *politics* can be singular or plural; *scissors* and *trousers* are always plural.

▶ <u>Physics</u> <u>requires</u> a great deal of studying.

Practice 8 Subject–Verb Agreement

In each sentence, circle the correct form of the **verb** and underline the **subject** with which the verb must agree.

▶ Today, the <u>group</u> ((decides)/decide) on the winner of the contest.

1. Each of the players (gives/give) an opinion, and then all of the team members (votes/vote).
2. Can viruses and worms (ruins/ruin) a person's hard drive?
3. Either a flatbed scanner or multifunction printer (is/are) a good addition to a home computer.
4. Coffee with biscotti (tastes/taste) good after dinner.
5. Everyone who is a member of the book club (loves/love) a good mystery book.
6. *Great Expectations* by Charles Dickens (is/are) read by many high school students.
7. Britain or other countries (is/are) providing the humanitarian aid.
8. Both of the weary parents (climbs/climb) the stairs to their third floor apartment.
9. None of the avocados that Margarita wanted to serve for dinner (is/are) ripe.
10. The group of software and management executives (attends/attend) each board meeting.

Pronoun Agreement and Ambiguous Reference

Subject–verb agreement is only one type of agreement that is essential in sentences. Pronouns must also agree with their antecedents. To understand pronoun reference or agreement, students must be familiar with the term *antecedent*, which is the noun that a pronoun either refers to or replaces. You may find pronoun agreement problems in sentences where students use pronouns that do not agree with their antecedents in person or number. Also, students create ambiguous references when the antecedents are not specific. When there is no specific antecedent, the use of pronouns such as *this, that, which*, and *it* create a broad, ambiguous meaning.

▶ *Faulty Ref:*   A parent is concerned about *their* child's grades in school.

   Revised: A parent is concerned about *his or her* child's grades in school.

   Revised: Parents are concerned about *their* child's grades in school.

[The sentence can be revised by changing either the pronoun or the subject.]

▶ *Ambiguous:*   The teacher gave an assignment to read a short story and to analyze its theme by the next class meeting, *which* the students felt was easy.

   Revised: The teacher gave an assignment to read a short story and to analyze its theme by the next class meeting; the students felt that *the assignment* was easy.

[Since the antecedent of the word *which* is not the noun *meeting*, the writer must reconstruct the dependent clause to eliminate the ambiguous reference.]

Helping students: When helping students with pronoun errors, make sure that

- every pronoun has a specific antecedent
- no ambiguous reference exists
- the pronoun agrees in number with its antecedent

When discussing subject–verb agreement, advise students that often it is easier to use all plural subjects, so that the plural pronouns *they, them*, and *their* can be used.

Practice 9 Pronoun Agreement

In the following sentences, correct any **pronoun agreement** or **reference** problems. Practice identifying the antecedents and verbalizing, as if in a tutoring session, the rules that apply and why each rule applies.

▶ Researchers tested a new cosmetic on mice and rabbits and found that there were no allergies to the dye. Activists said that *this* was inhumane.

Revision: Researchers tested a new cosmetic on mice and rabbits and found that there were no allergies to the dye. Activists said that *the tests were* inhumane.

1. Should a student revise their own essays, or should students take them to a learning center?
2. A penny saved is a penny earned; that is something we should do.
3. The Hippie Movement began in the 1960's because they rejected the "Establishment" and traditional American customs.
4. The slump in business activity may cause a recession, so this may cause the value of real estate to decline also.
5. Some people enjoy reading books on a hot summer day, and the library is a good place to find them.
6. Each dancer hopes that during a performance, they will make all the right moves.
7. Did everyone come prepared with their speech?
8. At the bank, when Mr. Wilson gave the man the money, he counted it two times.
9. We often go to the block-long mall because we like their stores and boutiques.
10. Each of the members must do their part on the committees.

Chapter 5

Sentence Building Blocks: Phrases, Clauses, and Sentences

You have already reviewed the eight parts of speech as well as subjects and verbs as sentence building blocks. Phrases and clauses are the other parts of sentences used to convey more developed and complex meanings. In this chapter, you will learn about

- participial, gerund, infinitive, and appositive phrases
- main (independent) clauses
- subordinate (dependent) clauses that include
    adjective clauses
    adverb clauses
    noun clauses

Phrases

A **phrase** does not contain a subject and a verb; instead, it is a group of words as in a prepositional phrase, participial phrase, gerund phrase, infinitive phrase, or appositive phrase.

1. A **prepositional phrase** contains a preposition plus a noun, noun phrase, or pronoun as the object of the preposition. Prepositions and prepositional phrases are covered in Chapter Three.

2. A **participial phrase** is a group of words that begins with either a present participle, the–*ing* form, or past participle, the –*ed* form that is used with the helping verbs *has, have,* or *had.* The entire participial phrase functions as an adjective modifier.

   ▶ *Riding swiftly,* Paul Revere warned fellow colonists of the British troops.

[The present participial phrase *riding swiftly* modifies the proper noun *Paul Revere*.]

▶ *Frightened by the thunder*, the little girl crawled into her mother's lap.

[The past participial phrase *frightened by the thunder* modifies the noun *girl*.]

3. A **gerund phrase** is a group of words that begins with a present participle, the–*ing* form, and functions in a sentence as a noun in one of several roles such as subject, direct object, or object of the preposition.

▶ *Learning four-part harmony* is important for a barbershop quartet. [subject]

▶ The barbershop quartet practices *singing four-part harmony*. [direct object]

▶ The barbershop quartet excels at *singing four-part harmony*. [object of prep]

4. An **infinitive phrase** is a group of related words that begins with the word *to* plus the base form of the verb. The entire infinitive phrase functions as a noun (as a subject, direct object, or subject complement), adjective, or adverb.

▶ *To work in the fashion industry* is her goal.   [noun as the subject]
▶ She wants *to work in the fashion industry*.   [noun as a direct object]
▶ Her goal is *to be as good* as she can be.   [noun as subject complement]
▶ She has a goal *to work in the fashion industry*.   [adjective]
▶ *To work in the fashion industry*, she has to have the right education. [adverb]

5. An **appositive phrase** is a group of words that describes or renames a noun or pronoun.

▶ Lana auditioned for <u>Rent</u>, *a Broadway show*.

Practice 10 *Identifying Types of Phrases*

Underline each **participial, gerund, infinitive**, or **appositive phrase** in the following sentences. Next, above the phrase, write the type of phrase. Then, for each gerund or infinitive phrase, determine its function.

    gerund   subject
▶ <u>Flying in an airplane</u> can be unnerving for some people because of innate fears.

1. To be able to write well is to be able to communicate.
2. Planning the plot, developing the characters, and creating the setting of a novel takes time and patience.
3. Oprah Winfrey's Book Club, a phenomenal success, has encouraged reading of books, both modern and classical.
4. Reading books while on vacation is enjoyable.
5. Kevin plans to read all the Harry Potter books.
6. Lin plans on reading *The Lord of the Rings* trilogy this summer.
7. The members of my family think that reading as many books as they can is valuable.
8. Every emerging novelist wants to write the great American novel.
9. The professor, a witty man, wrote two humor books when he retired.
10. Manuscripts typed on a word processor look better than manuscripts typed on an old-fashioned typewriter.

Clauses

Every **clause** must contain a subject and a verb. A clause can be either a complete sentence in itself or it may be a part of a larger sentence. **Main clauses**, also called **independent clauses**, express the important information of the sentence while **subordinate** or **dependent clauses** express less important ideas.

A **main** or **independent clause** is a group of words containing at least one subject and one verb that can stand on its own. A main clause expresses a complete thought or idea.

subject + verb = main clause

▶ The <u>technician</u> <u>fixed</u> the computer.

A **subordinate** or **dependent clause** is a group of words containing at least one subject and one verb that cannot stand on its own. A subordinate clause depends upon the main clause to complete the meaning of the subordinate clause. Either a **subordinate conjunction** or a **relative pronoun** introduces a dependent clause. **Adjective, adverb,** and **noun** clauses are the three types of dependent clauses.

1. **Adjective clauses** modify a noun or pronoun and are introduced by a relative pronoun: *that, which, who, whom, whose, whoever,* and sometimes *where* and *when.*

main clause   *adjective clause*

▶ The technician fixed the computer   purchased one month ago.

2. **Adverbial clauses** modify a verb, an adjective, or another adverb. These clauses show how, where, how much, or under what conditions. Adverbial clauses also can show comparison, manner, cause, result, degree, or purpose. Adverbial clauses are introduced by subordinating conjunctions such as *after, as, before, when, while, because, if, since, so that* and *although*. A list of subordinating conjunctions is also found in Chapter Three.

adverb clause	*main clause*

▶ When the computer's hard drive crashed, the technician fixed it.

3. **Noun clauses** begin with words such as *that, who, whom, whoever, whomever, what, whatever, when, where, whether, whose, why,* or *how*. Noun clauses function the same way that single word nouns function: as a subject, subject complement, direct object, or object of a preposition.

▶ *What he said in the deposition* became the basis for the testimony.
   [subject]
▶ The fundraiser will be *whatever the committee decides*.
   [subject complement]
▶ A conformist wears *whatever fashion all of his friends wear*.
   [direct object]
▶ His instructions were to give the reward to *whoever finds the lost dog*.
   [object of prep]

Practice 11 Identifying Types of Clauses

Underline each **subordinate clause** in the following sentences. Above the clause, write the type of clause: **adjective**, **adverb**, or **noun**. If a sentence contain no subordinate clause, do nothing.

   adverb clause
▶ Before the students arrived in class, the instructor had written the lecture notes on the board.

1. After eating, did the boy go swimming?
2. After the boy ate lunch, he went swimming.
3. When he went swimming, the boy who was unfamiliar with the lake went into the deep part.
4. Leah, because she wanted to impress Colin, purchased a new dress; however, when she tried it on for her mother, her mother did not approve of the dress.
5. What he wanted to say was not allowed.
6. She feared that the time was up.
7. Leave the money where no one will find it.

8. He didn't know anything about the crime except what the newspapers reported.
9. From a little after 11:00 A.M. until almost 5:00 P.M., the jurors sat in what all of them felt was a cramped sequester room because the judge, who was a stickler for following rules, did not want the jury approached by anyone who might be a media reporter.
10. The Beach Boys, who started singing in the 1960's, still perform at concerts where people of all ages enjoy their music.
11. You might think that this is a simple sentence, but it is not.
12. By the big oak tree in the dark woods near the little pond, stood the mansion.
13. Although my family thinks otherwise, I am a good cook.
14. Since complex sentences are interesting, we write many of them.
15. The meaning of the ambiguous reference is whatever the reader wants to make of it.

Sentences

Sentence Types

One element of strong writing is sentence variety that is accomplished by using a combination of main clauses and subordinate clauses (independent clauses and dependent clauses). When put together, these types of clauses form four different sentence types.

Simple sentence: One main (independent) clause containing at least one subject and verb.

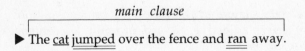

▶ The <u>cat</u> <u>jumped</u> over the fence and <u>ran</u> away.

Compound sentence: Two or more main (independent) clauses joined by a semicolon, a comma plus a coordinating conjunction, or semi-colon plus conjunctive adverb and a comma.

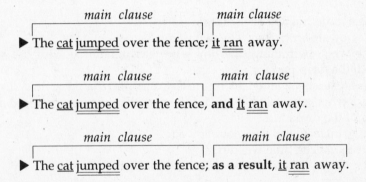

▶ The <u>cat</u> <u>jumped</u> over the fence; <u>it</u> <u>ran</u> away.

▶ The <u>cat</u> <u>jumped</u> over the fence, **and** <u>it</u> <u>ran</u> away.

▶ The <u>cat</u> <u>jumped</u> over the fence; **as a result,** <u>it</u> <u>ran</u> away.

Complex sentence: One main (independent) clause and at least one subordinate (dependent) clause.

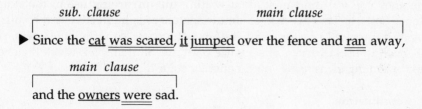

▶ Since the <u>cat was scared</u>, <u>it jumped</u> over the fence and <u>ran</u> away.

Compound-complex sentence: At least two main (independent) clauses and at least one subordinating (dependent) clause.

sub. clause   *main clause*

▶ Since the <u>cat was scared</u>, <u>it jumped</u> over the fence and <u>ran</u> away,

main clause

and the <u>owners were</u> sad.

When creating various types of sentences, writers are actually joining ideas and showing the relationship between those ideas. By using coordination and subordination to link and blend their ideas, writers not only show the importance of one idea over another but also make sentences more interesting.

Practice 12 Identification of Sentence Types

For each sentence, identify it as **simple**, **compound**, **complex**, or **compound-complex**.

▶ Since the gas prices have dropped, people have begun to spend more money on traveling. [complex]

1. In the Chinese theory of yin and yang, yin and yang represent the passive and active forces.
2. Because the car was so new, the owners felt that they had to exercise care in parking the car in large mall parking structures.
3. The girl had worked out for two hours in the gym; therefore, she was exhausted and sweaty.
4. While drawing a picture, Marie used her pastel colors so that the picture had a delicate quality about it; as a result, the artwork gave an impressionistic feeling.
5. Tea was served on the terrace, and all the ladies who met to discuss the new fundraiser enjoyed the afternoon gathering.
6. Can you identify an adverb clause, and can you identify a noun clause?
7. A midwife is not a physician but specializes in facilitating childbirth; an obstetrician is a physician who facilitates childbirth and other medical procedures.
8. Please close and lock the door.

9. Even though the sky is gray and cloudy, the temperature is warm today.
10. In the award-winning movie *Forrest Gump*, Gump is an example of a character who undergoes a transformation in his life.

Ways to Join Ideas and Create Effective Sentence Patterns: Coordination and Subordination

Sometimes you will find in student writing the unvarying use of the simple sentence pattern. This overuse of simple sentences is ineffective and results in an essay comprised of a series of choppy sentences. To write effectively, students need to use a variety of sentence patterns. Students can break the choppiness by joining ideas using coordination or subordination.

1. Coordination

Main clause, + coordinating conjunction + main clause.

▶ *The movie was good, but the book was better.*

Main clause; + main clause.

▶ *The movie was good; the book was better.*

Main clause; + conjunctive adverb (transitional expression) + main clause.

▶ *The movie was good; however, the book was better.*

2. Subordination

Main clause + subordinate clause.

▶ *The book was great although the movie was only good.*

Subordinate clause, + main clause.

▶ *Even though the movie was good, the book was better.*

Main clause subject, + subordinate clause, + main clause verb.

▶ *The movie, though it was good, wasn't as good as the book.*

Practice 13 Sentence Combining and Identification

Using **coordination** and **subordination**, combine each group of sentences into one **compound**, **complex**, or **compound-complex** sentence. Then identify the new sentence type.

▶ Ansel Adams was a famous American photographer. He took many black and white pictures. Many of them are of the West. Some of his most famous are of Yosemite. He also took photographs of the beautiful Redwoods.
Revision: Ansel Adams, who was a famous American photographer, took black and white pictures of the West that include his famous photographs of Yosemite and the beautiful Redwoods. [complex]

1. Megan's old car was put to shame. Megan saw her friend's restored 1968 Mustang. The Mustang had a new blue paint job.
2. The car's engine blew up. The mechanic's shop repaired the car's engine.
3. The ants crawled into the house. They appeared in the bedroom. The bedroom had to be sprayed for ants.
4. April in Paris is beautiful. Tourists love to go there. Many tourists visit the Eiffel Tower.
5. A lightening strike started the brush fire. The fire roared through the hills and burned over 10,000 acres in one day.
6. The large ship pulled into port yesterday. The passengers got off for two hours. They shopped in the tourist district.
7. Some might say that people with recognizable Hollywood names influence California politics. Ronald Reagan was governor of California. Sonny Bono was mayor of Palm Springs. Clint Eastwood was mayor of Carmel. Arnold Schwarzenegger is governor of California.
8. Many people listen to rock music. Country music is popular as well. Young people like rap music and hip-hop too.
9. Peggy Sue loved the song. It was played on a guitar. A rising country-rock star sang the song.
10. The Berlin Wall came down. The communist regime ended in 1989. Bonn had been West Germany's capital. Berlin is the capital of the unified country.

Chapter 6

Repairing Sentence Level Problems

Now that you have reviewed clauses and sentences, you will look at common writing errors. Besides acquainting basic level writers with these sentence problems, you can use many of these tips to help more advanced writers improve their tone and style. These types of repairs will help writers fine tune an essay or research paper. In this chapter you will review

- fragments, comma splices, and run-on sentences
- modifier problems: misplaced modifiers and dangling modifiers
- shifts in point of view and tense
- clarity in sentence construction

Fragments, Comma Splices, and Run-on Sentences

Three common grammatical errors that students make in their writing are fragmented sentences, comma splices, and run-on (fused) sentences. To avoid these errors, students need to remember that every main (independent) clause must have a subject and verb and express a complete thought while every subordinate (dependent) clause, though it too has a subject and verb, must be attached to a main clause to complete its meaning.

Fragments. A fragment is merely part of a sentence. The problem occurs when students do not include both a subject and verb in a sentence, when students use only the *–ing* form of the verb without an auxiliary verb, or when students have written only a dependent clause. To repair a fragment, students may need to

- add a missing subject, add a missing verb, or add both a missing subject and verb

- correct a verb problem
- add an independent clause to the dependent clause

The following examples show the three different types of fragments and the way to repair each type of fragment.

> *Fragment:*   Dances almost as well as Ginger Rogers.
> *Repair:*   **The young star** dances almost as well as Ginger Rogers.
> [add a subject]
> *Fragment:*   The young star dancing now in a hit Broadway play.
> *Repair:*   The young star **is** dancing now in a hit Broadway play.
> [repair the verb]
> *Fragment:*   Because the young star dances almost as well as Ginger Rogers. She is starring in a hit Broadway play.
> *Repair:*   Because the young star dances almost as well as Ginger Rogers, **she** is starring in a hit Broadway play.
> [join the clauses]

Comma splices and run-on sentences. These two sentence level problems are caused by the writer's inability to recognize the beginning and end of a complete thought or by the lack of correct punctuation. A comma splice is created when two main clauses are joined with a comma while the run-on sentence (also called a fused sentence) is created when two main clauses have no punctuation at all.

> *Comma splice:*   Susan bought three sweaters, all three sweaters cost $125.00.
> *Run-on sentence:*   Susan bought three sweaters all three sweaters cost $125.00.

Students can choose one of five ways to correct either a comma splice or run-on sentence. Using the above example, any one of the following ways will repair the error:

1. Insert a semicolon between the two main clauses.

   > *Repair:* Susan bought three sweaters; all three sweaters cost $125.00.

2. Insert a period after the first main clause, and capitalize the first word in the second main clause.

   > *Repair:* Susan bought three sweaters. **A**ll three sweaters cost $125.00.

3. Add a comma and a coordinating conjunction.

   > *Repair:* Susan bought three sweaters, **and** all three sweaters cost $125.00.

4. Add a semicolon, conjunctive adverb (or transitional expression), and a comma between the two main clauses.

   ▶ *Repair:* Susan bought three sweaters**; as a result,** she spent $125.00.

5. Create a subordinating clause and a main clause from the two clauses, and use proper punctuation if necessary.

   ▶ *Repair:* Susan bought three sweaters **that cost a total of $125.00.**

Helping students: When students ask you to help them on essays that contain fragments, comma splices, or run-ons, start with the basics: discussing subject and verbs. Ask students to read aloud the problem sentences and then find the subject(s) and verb(s) in sentences that need to be repaired.

- If either the subject or the verb or both are missing in a sentence fragment, ask students to supply the correct word(s) to complete the sentence.
- If, in a sentence fragment, students have used only the participle form, the –*ing* or –*ed* form of the verb without a helping verb, then discuss the formation of verb tenses.
- If students have written sentences that are comma splices or run-ons, list the ways to repair these problems.
- For sentence variety, encourage students to repair their sentences in a different manner each time.

Practice 14 Identification and Repair of Fragments, Comma Splices, and Run-on Sentences

In the following sentences, **identify** the type of error, and then **repair** any **fragments**, **comma splices**, or **run-on** sentences. Do nothing if the sentence is correct.

   ▶ I enjoyed seeing my parents last Sunday. Because I hadn't seen them in six months.
   Repair: I enjoyed seeing my parents last Sunday *because* I hadn't seen them in six months.

1. The saying "all's well that ends well." Also, the title of a Shakespearean play.
2. The Greeks won the Trojan War when they constructed an enormous hallow horse it became known as the Trojan Horse.
3. In their trick, the Greeks claimed that the horse was a gift to honor the goddess Athena, however the Greeks hid inside to sneak out later and sack Troy.
4. Can you come to the beach today or can you come tomorrow?

5. The firefighters racing down the street to make a rescue.
6. On top of the burning building standing ready to jump.
7. The firefighters climbed up the ladder, then they carried the man down.
8. Everyone on the ground cheered, the firefighters were heroes.
9. The man's family thankful for Engine Company 98.
10. Later Engine Company 98 had a special dinner the heroes were honored.
11. The Smithsonian exhibits the collection of inaugural gowns. Worn by the First Ladies.
12. Sit at the table.

Modifiers

Modifiers limit, change, alter, or describe other words. Modifiers can be single words, phrases, or clauses. A modifier functions as either an adjective or an adverb whether it is a word, phrase, or clause. Students can determine whether a modifier is an adjective or adverb by identifying the word being modified. For instance, if the word being modified is a noun or pronoun, the modifier is functioning as an adjective. If the word being modified is a verb, adjective, or adverb, then the modifier is functioning as an adverb. The following are two basic rules concerning modifiers:

- Modifiers need to be next to (or as close as possible to) the word being modified.
- Modifiers must modify something.

Misplaced modifier. Sometimes modifiers are used incorrectly because they are placed in the wrong position. To repair a misplaced modifier, the modifier, whether it is a single word or group of words, must be moved next to (or as close as possible to) the word that it modifies. When modifiers are used correctly, the writing becomes clearer.

> ▶ *Misplaced:* The gambler *almost* won two thousand dollars in one night at the casino.
> *Repair:* The gambler won *almost* two thousand dollars in one night at the casino.
> ▶ *Misplaced:* The cat slept in the chair *with long fur.*
> *Repair:* The cat *with long fur* slept in the chair.

Dangling modifier. A dangling modifier is defined as an introductory phrase (such as a participial phrase) that lacks a "doer" or performer (a noun or pronoun to be modified). Since modifiers must modify something, the introductory phrase ends up modifying the wrong noun. To repair this problem, the sentence must be rewritten to include the implied doer of the action. Just moving a dangling modifier will never repair the problem.

▶ *Dangling: Wanting to cross the river*, the inflatable raft was
                brought up to the dock.
   [Who wanted to cross the river? No "doer" of *wanting* exists.]
   Repair: Wanting to cross the river, the **boys** brought the
                inflatable raft up to the dock.

Helping students: When analyzing dangling modifiers, you should have
students identify the introductory phrase and the noun directly following the
phrase (the noun that follows after the comma). Ask students, "Can the noun
or pronoun directly following the verbal phrase do the implied action of the
verbal?" Remind students that a dangling modifier is an introductory phrase
that lacks a noun to modify.

Practice 15 Repair of Misplaced or Dangling Modifiers

In the following sentences, repair any **misplaced** or **dangling modifiers** by
moving the modifier to the correct place in the sentence or by rewriting the
sentence. Practice verbalizing how you would explain misplaced and dangling
modifiers to a student.

▶ Trapped in the woodshed, the father rescued his daughter's cat.
   Repair: The father rescued his daughter's cat that was trapped in the
   woodshed.

1. The elephant walked over the man that weighed three tons.
2. Driving all night, the car finally pulled into a motel.
3. Sherrie almost practiced the piano for twenty minutes.
4. Tanning her body, the sun felt good.
5. Skiing down the slope, the tree got in his way.
6. He nearly went twenty-five yards before he saw the tree.
7. To avoid the tree, the man's skis veered to the right.
8. The man approximately rolled down two hundred feet of the snow slope.
9. Trying to look in the window, the boy saw the little truck who was
   barely four feet tall.
10. Put the dress in the box that has been altered.

Shifts

Other common sentence problems are shifts that weaken the writing. You
should look for two types of shifts: shifts in point of view and shifts in verb
tense.

1. **Point of view shifts.** Students may write essays in one of three points of
   view:

First person: I, we
Second person: you
Third person: he or she, they, it

Shifts occur when writers start in one point of view, for instance third person, and then use another point of view, for instance second person, later in the sentence or in the next sentence(s).

▶ *Shift:*   When the children got to the party, you could see many colorful decorations.
  Repair: When the children got to the party, they could see many colorful decorations.

Along with *he*, *she*, *they*, and *it*, words such as *person*, *people*, and *one* are considered third person.

2. **Tense shifts**. This type of shift occurs when writers change from one tense to another without a specific reason for the shift. For instance, writers may start essays with the first sentence in the present tense and then shift to past tense in the next clause or sentence without any indication of a shift in the time frame.

▶ *Shift:*   Gandhi *was* a famous leader in India until he *is* assassinated in 1948.
  Repair: Gandhi *was* a famous leader in India until he *was* assassinated in 1948.

Helping students: Remind students of the basic rule: Writers should remain in one tense and use one point of view unless a specific reason exists to shift the tense or the point of view.

The Literary Present Point of View

When writing about literature or the arts, students often have trouble with shifts in tense. Essays about literature should be in the present tense because literature still lives in the present time of the reader. Students should write, "Romeo <u>says</u>" rather than "Romeo <u>said</u>," or students should claim that "the theme of *Romeo and Juliet* <u>is</u> . . ." rather than "the theme of *Romeo and Juliet* <u>was</u> . . ." This writing about literature or the arts in the present tense is called the "literary present."

The problem of shifts using the literary present arises when students include historical or biographical information that actually did occur in the past or when students need to show a past action in the story, poem, or drama that they are critiquing or discussing. For such a purpose, a shift in tense is appropriate. Edgar V. Roberts, in *Writing about Literature*, provides an excellent demonstration of this tense shift in a sample paragraph about *Hamlet*. Roberts writes:

> Because *Hamlet* **was** first performed in about 1600, Shakespeare most probably **wrote** it shortly before this time. In the play, a tragedy, Shakespeare **treats** an act of vengeance, but more importantly he **demonstrates** the difficulty of ever learning the exact truth. The hero, Prince Hamlet, **is** the focus of this difficulty, for the task of revenge **is assigned** to him by the Ghost of his father. Though the Ghost **claims** that his brother, Claudius, **is** his murderer, Hamlet **is** not able to verify this claim.[1]

Roberts uses bold font for the verbs so that the reader can easily see the shift from past to present. Notice that the historical or biographical information is written in the past while the discussion about the events in the play is rendered in the present tense. This shift from past to present and back again is a permissible shift.

Helping students: Often in their writing, you will find that students appropriately shift in some spots but then begin to shift back and forth without reason. The rules to follow are simple.

- Literary essays or critiques about literature or the arts should be, overall, written in the literary present. The information to be written in the present tense includes the actions and ideas found in the work being discussed.
- Shifts in tense, from present to past to present, are permissible when an incident in the story, poem, drama, or work of art occurs in the past. Additionally, the shift to past tense is appropriate when the past tense is required to show the logical flow of events or when historical or biographical information is being provided.

Practice 16 *Repair of Shifts*

Correct any shifts in point of view or tense in the paragraph below. Several different repairs are possible. In a practice tutoring session, verbalize the types of shifts and how to repair them.

> Known as the "cowboy artist," Charles M. Russell was born in 1865. Having lived in the West during the last half of the nineteenth century and early twentieth century, he sees the West of the great cattle drives and the country where Lewis and Clark go up the Missouri River. As an artist of the Old West, Russell visualized for you what no words could express. One of his most famous sketches was "The Last of the Five Thousand" that depicted the winter of 1886–1887 when thousands of cattle are dying in the freezing weather. His sketch was showing the

effect that the cold winter is having on the cattle industry in Montana. Charles Russell also paints or sketches pictures of the American Indian. One of his paintings depicted the Lewis and Clark Expedition led by Sacajawea when the group meets the Flathead Indians in the Bitterroot Mountains. Russell also was an illustrator for calendars and magazines, but today he is best known for his large-scale paintings that illustrated the Old West.

Helping Students to Write with Clarity and to Construct Smooth, Flowing Sentences

Students will be able to write with **clarity** and to construct smooth, flowing sentences if they know how to avoid **wordiness** and **awkward sentences** and if they use the **active voice** as well as **concrete words** and **thoughts**. Furthermore, **logical connections** between thoughts within a sentence and between sentences produce clarity and a well-written paragraph or essay. Finally, for well-constructed sentences, students should use **coordination** and **subordination** as well as **transitional expressions**.

Producing clarity in sentences. You can help students write sentences that have clarity by showing them how to avoid wordy and awkward sentences. Explain to students how to use active voice instead of passive voice, how to use concrete words, how to revise choppy sentences, and how to make logical connections.

Wordiness. When a thought can be conveyed in fewer words or revised for conciseness, a sentence is considered wordy. When helping students with wordy sentences you can do the following:

- Look for unnecessary redundancy, repetition, and meaningless phrases.
- Look for wordy phrases such as *due to the fact that* which can be replaced with *because.*
- Look for the excessive use of prepositional phrases. Often these phrases can be redrafted as adjective or adverbial clauses, verbal phrases, or single word modifiers.

> ▶ *Wordy:*   The Senate searched *for proof of fault for the violation of the terms of the treaty.*
>
> *Revised:*   The Senate searched for proof to determine who violated the treaty's terms.

Awkward sentences. When students begin sentences with one type of construction and then switch to another type of construction in the middle, the sentences become awkward. For instance, sentences are awkward when constructed with words such as *is where, one reason . . . is because, one situation . . . is when.* These sentences should be revised for conciseness.

▶ *Awkward:*   *One reason* that many trees died during the recent
             drought *is because* of bark beetle infestation.
Revised: During the recent drought, many trees died because of
             bark beetle infestation.

Sometimes sentences are awkward because a student has written a noun clause
as the subject, but the noun clause is long and awkward. Help students analyze
the awkward sentences and untangle the noun clause to create a meaningful
subject.

▶ *Awkward:*   *That the recent environmental emergency was a reason*
             to declare a disaster was an action item on the board's I
             agenda.
Revised: One action item on the board's agenda declared the
             recent environmental emergency a disaster.

Active voice versus passive voice. Active voice sentences will lead to strong,
meaningful ideas, and the sentences will be less wordy than passive voice
sentences. The use of passive voice can lead to unclear sentences because students omit the "doer" of the action, or they put the actual "doer" of the action
in a prepositional phrase. You will need to brainstorm with students to identify the doer of the action in the sentence; then students can rewrite the
sentence in the active voice. The use of active versus passive voice is also
explained in Chapter Four.

Concrete words and thoughts. Students should avoid starting sentences with
words such as *there is* or *there are*. Encourage students to use concrete words or
concepts in place of broad reference words such as *it, what, that, which,* and
this when the words have no direct antecedent. These words must refer to some
specific noun that immediately precedes the pronoun. *What, that, which* and
this cannot refer to a phrase or clause.

▶ The United States has always welcomed immigrants from other
  countries. *This* has led to the diversity of culture in this country.
  Revised: The United States has always welcomed immigrants from
  other countries. *Immigration over the years* has led to the diversity of
  culture in this country.

The word *this* in the first example sentence has no direct antecedent; instead,
the word *this* refers to the entire clause in the previous sentence. In the
revised sentence, a concrete noun has been inserted to replace the broad reference of the word *this*.

Choppy sentences. By combining choppy sentences, students can write smooth,
flowing ones.

▶ It was five o'clock. Grace had to fix dinner. She left her neighbor's
  house.

Though the ideas are clear, the sentences are choppy. To create smooth, flowing sentences, choppy sentences can easily be combined through the use of both subordination and coordination.

> *Revised:* Since it was five o'clock, Grace had to fix dinner, so she left her neighbor's house.

> *Revised:* Because she had to fix dinner, Grace left her neighbor's house at five o'clock.

Either one of the two revisions clearly establishes the relationship between the ideas, producing a more coherent and interesting sentence.

Logical connections. To achieve logical connections in a paragraph, all supporting sentences must relate to the essay's central idea and to the main point of the paragraph. The first step is to have a strong topic sentence with one main idea for each paragraph. Every sentence in a particular paragraph must relate to the point indicated in the topic sentence. For instance, in paragraph A, students should discuss only point A. Students should not discuss three different points if the topic sentence indicates the paragraph will discuss only point A. Also, help students to identify where they have a jump in thought and have omitted pertinent or necessary information or where they drift onto tangents that do not support the paragraph.

Practice for Clarity and Flow

Read the paragraph below; rewrite to provide clarity and smooth, flowing sentences. Revisions may vary. Also, you might use this paragraph for a practice tutoring session.

> The Cherokee Indians were one of the first Native American tribes to be known as a "civilized" tribe. They were known as a "civilized" tribe because in the early 1800's, some of the Cherokees felt that they needed to live more like the white people in order to survive. This was also because they wanted to retain their ancestral homelands in the Southeast United States. To help in this "civilization" process, some of the mixed-ancestry Cherokee leaders invited some white people into their nation to help educate Cherokee children. In order to help the Cherokees in this "civilization" process, the United States government encouraged missionaries from the New England states to travel to the Cherokee Nation. The missionaries established schools. Many Cherokee children were educated at these boarding schools. They learned the English language. Girls learned domestic skills. Boys learned about agriculture. Girls learned how to sew and spin yarn. They learned how to cook. Another reason that the Cherokees were known as a "civilized" tribe is because a Cherokee by the name of Sequoyah invented a syllabary for

the Cherokee language. He could not read English. He wrote down symbols. Some looked like the English alphabet. Some looked like Greek letters. He wrote these on leaves. His 86 symbols became the Cherokee syllabary. Sequoyah's syllabary was introduced to the Cherokees. They were able to learn to read and write in a matter of weeks. There was a newspaper, the *Cherokee Phoenix*. It was first published in 1828. In the newspaper, news of their nation could now be read by the Cherokees in their own language. In it, Cherokee laws were read by them. They could read about people in other parts of the United States. There are several reasons the Cherokees were known as a "civilized" tribe. Two of the reasons the Cherokees were known as a civilized tribe is because of the girls and boys receiving an education and because of the invention of the Cherokee syllabary.

Chapter 7

Punctuation, Mechanics, and Words

In this chapter, you will review punctuation rules as well as review tips to help students with word usage. It is important for students to learn and use correct punctuation because those little marks communicate information to the reader. Sometimes, if the punctuation is incorrect, the meaning of a sentence can change the idea that the writer intended to convey. Because grammar books contain detailed explanations, this guide will focus on a few of the areas which are most problematic for students:

- commas
- semicolons
- spelling out numbers
- words often confused
- words to avoid

When you are comfortable with punctuation explanations, you can be effective in tutoring students to locate their own errors and to use commas and semicolons correctly.

Helping Students with Punctuation and Mechanics

Commas

1. **Use a comma before a coordinating conjunction** (*but, or, yet, so, for, and, nor*) that joins two main clauses.

   ▶ George likes to ride a bicycle to save on gasoline**,** but sometimes he drives a car in bad weather.

When a coordinating conjunction joins two main clauses, a comma must be placed before the coordinating conjunction. However, when a coordinating conjunction joins two subjects or two verbs or other multiple word groups, no comma is used.

▶ The blue car suddenly appeared, and the other car's driver swerved to avoid it.
  [The comma is necessary because *and* is joining two main clauses.]
▶ The blue car suddenly appeared and drove on.
  [No comma is necessary to join two verbs.]

2. **Use a comma with three or more items in a series.**

▶ Lincoln, Wilson, Roosevelt, and Truman were all wartime presidents.

3. **Use a comma between two or more adjectives in a series** if the word *and* can be placed between the adjectives or the order of the adjectives can be reversed without changing the meaning. However, if *and* cannot be placed between the adjectives or the order cannot be reversed, no commas should be placed between adjectives.

▶ He was a smart, energetic man.   [comma necessary]
▶ The man wore a black leather jacket.   [no comma necessary]

4. **Use a comma with introductory items** at the beginning of a sentence.

• After introductory words:

  ▶ Yes, a lunar eclipse occurred this year.

• After introductory prepositional phrases:

  ▶ *After the hurricane of 1998, the town had to be rebuilt.*

For a short prepositional phrase, the comma may be optional if no confusion exists. However, some grammar books and instructors recommend that a comma be placed after all introductory prepositional phrases, so students should defer to the direction of their instructors.

• After introductory participial phrases:

  ▶ Filmed at the Hotel del Coronado, *Some Like It Hot* is a classic comedy.

- After introductory adverb clauses:

  ▶ When the telemarketer called, I was eating dinner.

Punctuation note: When an adverbial clause is placed before the main clause, a comma is necessary after the adverbial clause. When an adverbial clause is placed after a main clause, in most instances no comma is necessary. If an adverbial clause is placed in the middle of the sentence, usually between the subject and verb, commas are placed before and after the adverbial clause.

5. **Use a comma to set off** words such as *he said*. Also, quotation marks are used around the words that are the dialogue with commas and periods inside the quotation marks.

   ▶ Jorge said, "The vines will produce good wine this year."
   ▶ "The vines will produce good wine this year," Jorge said.

6. **Use a comma with interrupters.**

   - With nonrestrictive phrases or clauses (phrases or clauses that are not essential for the meaning of the sentence):

     ▶ Isabel, who is always late, finally called a taxi.
       [adjective clause]
     ▶ Rochelle, sitting patiently at home, waited for Isabel.
       [participial phrase]

   - With appositive phrases:

     ▶ Mrs. Schmidt, a good cook, bakes delicious apple pies.

   - With parenthetical expressions such as *however, for example, finally, in fact:*

     ▶ The pie, however, is not as good as the one she baked last month.

   - With direct address:

     ▶ Tina, I hope you remember that we are leaving at 11:00 A.M.
     ▶ I hope you remember, Tina, that we are leaving at 11:00 A.M.

   - With words that express contrast:

     ▶ Dogs, unlike people, are loyal.

With interrupters, if a word, phrase, or clause can be removed from a sentence without altering the meaning of the sentence, then that word, phrase, or clause should be set off by (placed between) commas.

7. **Use a comma in dates.**

   ▶ On June 13, 1995, I got married.

8. **Use a comma in addresses** (not between state and zip code).

   ▶ John Smith, 1345 N Street, Small Town, New York 10001

9. **Use a comma in the salutation in a personal letter.**

   ▶ Dear Aunt Betty,

10. **Use a comma to close a business or personal letter.**

    ▶ Sincerely, Richard Jones
    ▶ Love, Sally

Semicolons

1. **Use a semicolon to join two main clauses** (independent clauses) that are closely related in thought.

   ▶ The volcano erupted wildly; the villagers fled for their lives.

   Remind students not to overuse semicolons. A string of main clauses connected with semicolons leads to a redundancy of style. Students should use a variety of ways to connect main thoughts to include using coordination and subordination.

2. **Use a semicolon with conjunctive adverbs** (transitional expressions) such as *therefore* or *consequently* that link two main clauses.

   ▶ The volcano erupted wildly; consequently, the villagers fled for their lives.

3. **Use semicolons in place of commas when other intervening commas exist** such as in a list of items.

   ▶ My mother, an attorney; my brother, an artist; my sister, unmarried; and my father, a professor, all live in the same house.

For other specific punctuation rules, consult a grammar book.

Spelling Out Numbers

Because differences exist in the usage of numerals or words for numbers, consult the grammar book that the student is using for his or her class to determine the acceptable rule. In most cases, these rules apply.

- If the number can be spelled out in two words, write the number as words: *twenty-two*. Remember to use a hyphen for compound numbers between twenty-one and ninety-nine.
- If the number requires three words, use numerals: *354* (instead of *three hundred fifty-four*).
- Look for consistency. When several numbers need to be written as numerals in the essay, report, letter, or research paper, be consistent and use all numerals.
- If a number is the first word of a sentence, spell out the number or rewrite the sentence.

Practice 18 Repair of Punctuation and Mechanical Errors

Correct the punctuation in the following sentences. Also, use these sentences in a practice tutoring session explaining applicable rules and encouraging your "tutee" to make revisions.

1. Melissa saved $800.00 in 6 months therefore she had money to buy the dining room set.
2. After his release from prison Nelson Mandela was elected President of South Africa and he also won a Nobel Peace Prize.
3. On June 13 2003 the family gathered for an engagement party.
4. It never snows in Death Valley it gets scorching hot in the summer.
5. Arlene said "It's so cold please close the door".
6. Do you want to help on the food line or do you want to hand out blankets?
7. Sydney when he is tired will rest only in the comfort of a snugly chair.
8. He will however sleep on a bed at night.
9. Cats unlike dogs are independent.
10. Adverbs can modify verbs adjectives or other adverbs.

Words Often Confused

The following list contains some words often confused by writers. For a more comprehensive list, refer to a grammar handbook. Remind students to carefully check the use of these words in their essays because spell checkers do not identify this type of error.

Word	Explanation	Sentence Example
affect **effect**	*to affect* is an action verb *the effect* is a noun	This new law *affects* all people. The *effect* on the people was enormous.
a lot	two words, but avoid the two words *a lot* and find a more concrete word and rewrite.	*A lot* of people enjoy beach vacations. *Many* people enjoy beach vacations.
another **other**	means one more of means the last one in a specific group or the only one that remains	I would like *another* serving, please. The *other* lawnmower works well.
its **it's**	possessive pronoun contraction for the two words *it is*	The cat licks *its* paw. *It's* a beautiful day.
lay **lie**	the act of putting something down reclining	Hens *lay* eggs. *Lay* the book on the table. Sharon *lies* on the bed to read.
that **which**	for clauses essential to the meaning of the sentence (clauses not set off with commas) for clauses not essential for the meaning of the sentence (clauses set off with commas)	The car *that* belongs to Joe is not running. Joe's car, *which* is red, is not running.
there **their** **they're**	refers to a place a possessive pronoun a contraction for *they are*	The family living over *there* is on vacation. When the family was gone, *their* house was robbed. *They're* sad because the VCR was stolen.
to **too** **two**	preposition showing direction or place adverb meaning *also, excessively,* or *in addition* the number 2	I am going *to* class. She was *too* tired to go hiking. I have *two* errands that I will do later.

Word	Explanation	Sentence Example
where	refers to a place	National Parks are places *where* people go to see beautiful scenery.
were	past tense verb of *to be*	Several spectacular roses *were* at the flower show.

Words to Avoid

Remind students that the use of the following words leads to lack of clarity and weak sentences. Although the one time use of any of these words is not a serious flaw in an essay, the excessive use of any of these words does lead to weak repetition.

- *it, it seems*
- *there is, there are, there was, there were, there will be*
- *like, really, very, thing, just, a lot, a lot of*
- *well* as an introductory word in a sentence
- over use of *to be* verbs: *am, is, was, were, be, being, been*
- *you*—the use of the second person point of view other than in a "how-to" essay

Practice 19 Words Often Confused and Words to Avoid

Correct any often confused words or words to avoid in the paragraph below. Also, you might use this paragraph in a practice tutoring session.

Today, their are alot of popular clubs to which car enthusiasts belong. One kind is the Early Ford V-8 Club. It's members own Fords built between 1932 and 1953. Other one is the Mustang Club were it's members own classic Mustangs. Well, the affect of having popular car clubs seems to be that old Fords are now being restored were in years past, you found that many cars were just sold to the wrecking yards. These clubs provide a social outlet for there members to. There are very nice things like ice cream socials, classic car nights, and day trips in caravans. The only bad thing about owning a classic car is the difficulty of finding parts to repair the old cars; however, belonging to a car club and meeting other owners helps when you need to locate car parts.

Chapter 8

Helping Multilingual and ESL Students

Both native and non-native speakers may have problems with proper English phrases, clauses, sentence patterns, and sentence structure. However, ESL students must learn to write and think in the English language. As a result, they may need extra help in certain areas such as:

- sentence patterns and sentence structure
- idiomatic expressions
- articles
- prepositions
- verbs including tense, aspect, agreement, and modality
- the concept of plagiarism

Linguistically, languages have different structures. ESL students bring to their learning of the English language the word formation as well as the phrase, clause, and sentence structure patterns of their native language. For example, if a student's native language, such as Japanese and Russian, does not use articles, then that student may have problems learning the English article system. Even though it helps to be familiar linguistically with the students' languages, you do not have to learn their language in order to help ESL students with their writing. Rather, you should be familiar with the differences between students' native languages and English to be more sensitive to their writing problems.[1]

Material presented in this chapter will help in tutoring ESL students and help in learning more about their problems with language and words. Also, refer to available resources such as ESL textbooks, ESL sections of grammar handbooks, and dictionaries geared towards ESL students. These dictionaries have special ESL material.[2]

Sentence Pattern, Sentence Structure, and Word Order

Writing structurally sound sentences and paragraphs can be difficult for ESL writers. As you help them, you will find that they have problems with sentence patterns, structure, and word order; often when they have a sentence to write, they think of the words and sentence patterns in their own language.

Sentence Patterns

To aid them as they choose words and write sentences, many ESL writers take out their electronic dictionaries and translate the vocabulary words using the sentence structure and word order in which the words are understood in their native language. For instance, a Japanese student might want to write a sentence that in English should say:

> *subject   verb   direct object*
> ▶ <u>Airlines</u> <u>have taken</u> more security precautions.

Because the Japanese language has a subject-object-verb (SOV) sentence structure, a Japanese student who does direct translation from his or her native language into English might end up writing the above sentence as:

> *subject   direct object   verb*
> ▶ <u>Airlines</u> more security precautions <u>have taken</u>.

Notice that the subject is mentioned first, then the object, and the verb is last in this direct-translation sentence. This SOV pattern creates problems of comprehension for other readers because those readers are expecting the English sentence structure based on the subject-verb-object (SVO) sentence pattern.

Sentence Structure

- ESL students often create faulty English sentence structure because of the word *there*. *There* in English is used to show that something exists or happens, or it is used to indicate a location. Students who do not have this type of word in their native language have a tendency to leave the word *there* out of a sentence.

> ▶ Everyday are many families vacationing at Disneyland.

A native speaking reader would identify the above group of words as either a question or a fragment.

▶ *Revised*: Everyday there are many families vacationing at Disneyland.

- Another problem is the repetition of the subject. Some students insert a pronoun that agrees with the subject that has already been named.

▶ Many families they take vacations at Disneyland.

You should point out to students that each sentence needs only one subject.

- ESL students have problems with phrases and clauses because they may not be comfortable using connecting words such as *however* to join thoughts. In addition, they may also leave out a preposition such as *in* or *by*, or they may leave out a subordinating conjunction such as *if* or *when*. Sometimes a student may even leave out a coordinating conjunction such as *and* or *but*. In classes, ESL students are learning how to correctly use subordinating conjunctions, conjunctive adverbs, and coordinating conjunctions, so use the actual terminology when you are discussing connectors with them.

- Students often use *and*, *but*, *so*, and other coordinating conjunctions to begin a sentence. However, ESL students are taught that coordinating conjunctions join two main clauses, so remind them not to use a coordinating conjunction as the first word in a sentence.

Word Order

Word order in the English language can be perplexing depending on the pattern with which students are familiar in their native language.

- **Adjective placement**. Adjectives that describe, such as *big*, *small*, and *red*, are called attributive adjectives. These adjectives come before the noun that the adjectives modify, for example, *an intelligent teacher*. For the English speaker, the adjectives *an* and *intelligent* come before the noun *teacher*; however, in Spanish, adjectives go after the noun that they modify as in *maestro inteligente*. Since the placement of words that modify nouns is problematic for ESL students, the following chart may help you explain the prescribed order of some cumulative adjectives.

Deter-miners	Opinion adjective	Physical size	Description age	Adjectives nationality	Modifier	Noun
the	intelligent		young		English	tutor
my	battered	little	old		grammar	book
an	educated	tall	middle-aged	Canadian	company	CEO
one	talented		teenaged	Irish	rock	star

Note that the above chart does not pretend to be exhaustive; it simply exemplifies the fact that English cumulative adjectives have a fixed word order.

• **Adverb placement**. Adverbs are another difficult area. Although adverbs can be placed in several places in a sentence, they too have some fixed spots where they are used. If an ESL student uses his or her native language word order for adverbs, the result is often an awkward sounding sentence in English. For example, German speakers commonly place an adverbial modifier between the verb and the object.

▶ We bought *in the morning* a car.

This placement, in English, sounds awkward. For correct English sentence structure, the prepositional phrase modifier in this sentence should appear in one of two locations.

▶ We bought a car *in the morning*.   [after the noun *car*]
▶ *In the morning*, we bought the car.   [at the beginning of the sentence]

Idioms

An **idiom** is a group of words that in a particular order has a special or different meaning than the meaning of the words individually.

▶ He had to *rack his brains* to figure out the equation.

In the above sentence, the idiom *rack his brains* means to think intensely about something. Usually, the words grouped as an idiom cannot be taken apart or changed, for the meaning is then changed. Along with an ESL textbook that discusses idioms, *The American Heritage Dictionary of Idioms for Students of English*, *The American Heritage English as a Second Language Dictionary*, and *The Longman Advanced American Dictionary* all have excellent coverage about idioms specifically for the ESL student.

Practice 20: Idiomatic Expressions

Each sentence below contains an **idiomatic expression**. First, highlight or underline the idiom; then, without using a dictionary, try explaining the expression as you would to an ESL student.

1. Richard wanted to buy a digital camera, so he should give it a whirl.

_____

2. Even though she went bankrupt, Priscilla tried to keep up with the Joneses.

_____

3. I went on a trip down memory lane.

_____

4. The odds are stacked against the team.

_____

5. The stock market was up, so the investor felt he should strike while the iron is hot.

_____

Articles

ESL students are learning important grammatical concepts about the English system of articles. If you are a native speaker, you may not be familiar with details of this article system such as

- count and noncount nouns
- *the* as the definite article
- *a* and *an* as indefinite articles
- no article used in certain indefinite situations

Articles are either the definite article *the* or indefinite articles *a* or *an*. In general, the definite article *the* is used to identify and specify, and the indefinite articles *a* and *an* are used to classify and generalize. English and other languages that have an article system use these function words to mark whether a noun has definite or indefinite, countable or uncountable (noncount), singular or plural meaning. Acquiring the ability to use this complex system requires diligent study and years of practice for ESL students.

Count and Noncount Meaning

Knowing whether a noun has either count or noncount meaning is essential for students who are trying to learn English article usage.

- A countable noun means that you can count the items, such as *four oranges* or *two cars*. If a noun is countable, you can add *–s* or *–es* to the noun to form the plural as in *two cars*.
- A noncount noun refers to something—a mass, an abstract concept, or a collection—that cannot be counted, such as *salt, sugar, rice, knowledge, information, water,* or *jealousy*. A noncount noun has no plural form; you do not say *rices* or *knowledges*. You usually cannot use the article *a* or *an* with a noncount noun.

The Definite Article the

- If the specific noun can be identified, then the definite article *the* is used. This noun in context must be specific and identifiable.

  ▶ We want to eat at *the* new steak restaurant on A Street.
  [*The* is used because one identifiable new steak restaurant is located on that specific street.]

- A countable singular noun must have an article (or another appropriate noun marker such as *this, my, John's*) preceding it. The function of the definite article is to point to the noun that is specific and identifiable.

  ▶ I am going to buy *the* DVD player that Wal Mart has on sale.
  [Wal Mart has one, identifiable DVD player that fits this specific description.]

- Plural proper nouns (the Giants), union names (the United Kingdom), and proper names containing identifying phrases (the Gulf of Mexico) all require the definite article *the*.

  ▶ I saw *the* Rolling Stones in concert ten years ago.

The Indefinite Articles a and an

- Indefinite articles classify and generalize. If you cannot identify the specific noun or if the noun has a general meaning, then use the indefinite article *a* or *an*.

▶ We are dining out at *a* restaurant for dinner. Also, I want to go to *a* rock concert.
[The specific restaurant or concert is not known.]

• When the indefinite noun is singular with count meaning, remind ESL students that *a* is used before consonant sounds, and *an* is used before vowel sounds.

▶ Tim has to write *an essay* before next Tuesday.
▶ Bianca is going to purchase *a new* car.

Note that a word such as *university* starts with the vowel *u*, but the sound of the *u* is a *y*-sound—a consonant sound; thus the article *a* is used.

▶ I am going to *a university* this fall, but I don't know which one yet.

No Article

Specific situations exist when no article is needed. Often students mistakenly insert an article, and you will need to explain why no article is needed.

• With noncount nouns that have an indefinite meaning, use no article.

▶ Students attend *college* to attain *knowledge* about various subjects.
▶ *Rice* is a staple food in many Asian countries.

• Use no article with generalizations about a countable noun in the plural form.

▶ *Bears* often attack garbage *cans* in *campgrounds*.

[All the nouns are generalizations. The reader does not know which specific bears, which specific garbage cans, or which specific campgrounds.]

• Normally use no article with singular proper nouns: Disneyland, Juan, Alicia, New York, Los Angeles, Mars.

The following dialogue exemplifies the **subsequent mention** rule. When the noun is introduced, use an indefinite article; however, when the same noun is used again, use the definite article.

A. Question: Do you live in *a house* or *an apartment*?	The exact house or apartment is unknown at this point, so the indefinite article is used.
B. Answer: I live in *a house*.	The exact or definite house still has not been identified, so the indefinite article is still used.
A. Question: Where is *the house* located?	Using the subsequent mention rule, the article now changes to the definite article *the* because both A. and B. have identified the same house, B.'s house.
B. Answer: *The house* is located in Los Angeles, California.	B. uses the definite article *the* because both A. and B. have already identified the house.
A. Question: Is *your house* furnished?	Instead of an article, A. uses a possessive pronoun.
B. Answer: Yes, I have *furniture*.	B. uses no article because B. is introducing furniture in general terms.
A. Question: Is *the furniture* new?	A. uses the definite article *the* because A. is using the subsequent mention rule referring to B.'s identified furniture.
B. Answer: Yes, *the furniture* is new.	B. continues to use the definite article *the*.

Helping students: If an ESL student's first language does not use articles, then that student will probably struggle with articles, so it is important to explain articles as simply as possible.

▶ I bought *car* last week.

In the above sentence, the student has left out the indefinite article before the noun *car*, so start by asking the student *what* he or she bought last week. The student will either self-correct and say *a car*, or repeat the error and say *car*. If the student repeats the error, ask the student how many cars. The student obviously will say *one car*. Tell the student that the indefinite articles *a* and *an* are derived from the word *one*. Omitting an indefinite article *a* or *an* or the definite article *the* is the most frequently made article error.

▶ I had to go to *library* after class.

With this article error, ask the student *which* library he or she had to go to after class. The student should be able to immediately correct the error by saying *the library*. Leading students to engage in self-correction rather than spoon-feeding them answers is the most effective way to tutor all students. The following flow chart will help students to determine which article to use with a common noun.

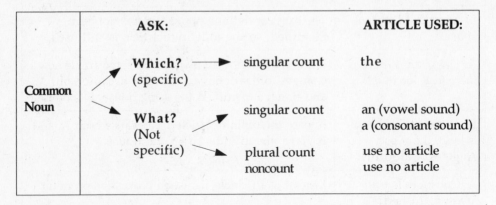

	ASK:		ARTICLE USED:
Common Noun	**Which?** (specific) →	singular count	the
	What? (Not specific) →	singular count	an (vowel sound) a (consonant sound)
		plural count noncount	use no article use no article

While the above flow chart will help students determine article use for common nouns, the next chart and list will aid students in determining article use for proper nouns because some proper nouns function like common nouns when determining article use.

Use no article before proper nouns that indicate	Use *the* before a proper noun that
a person, city, county, state, country, continent, lake, mountain, park, bay, island, holiday, or street	is plural; has an identifying phrase like a prepositional phrase (the Leaning Tower of Pisa); is a union, river, canal, aqueduct, ocean, desert, bridge, hotel, drama theater, museum, newspaper, or famous ship

▶ Courageous people climb *Mount Everest* each year.   [no article]
▶ *Shelly* obtained a job as a tour guide last week.   [no article]
▶ When I drive to San Francisco, I have to cross *the Golden Gate Bridge*. [definite article]

Some proper nouns can function as common nouns. The following proper noun categories can function in this manner:

days of the week   months of the year   family members
religions   political parties   products   franchises

▶ Winter break occurs in *December* and *January*.
[Months of the year function as proper nouns.]

▶ If you take a day off on *a Friday*, you will have a nice three-day weekend.
[Day of the week functions as a common noun with indefinite meaning.]

▶ If you take *the next Friday* off, the weather should be good for a three-day trip.
[Day of the week functions as a common noun with definite meaning.]

Practice 21: Use of Articles

Fill in the blank with the appropriate **article**: *the, a, an*, or *no* (for no article needed). Practice using the common noun flow chart or the proper noun charts to determine article use.

1. What does _____ Rhonda do? She is _____ English teacher.
2. _____ dogs hate _____ cats.
3. _____ Giants lost to _____ Dodgers.
4. _____ State of California is having _____ economic problems.
5. _____ young people come to _____ United States to get _____ education
6. _____ United Nations is _____ international organization.
7. _____ Pilgrims planned _____ feast to celebrate their survival in _____ colony at _____ Plymouth.
8. _____ people traveling on _____ airplane should plan on arriving at ____ airport two to two and a half hours before _____ time of _____ departure.

Prepositions

Prepositions are difficult for ESL students for five reasons.

1. The English language has many prepositions, more than many other languages. The language contains so many different kinds of prepositions: one-word (*in*), compound (*into*), two-word (*because of*), three-word (*in spite of*), and even four-word prepositions (*as a result of*). English prepositions can be classified as simple prepositions like *in, on, at*; compound prepositions like *into, onto, upon*; and complex prepositions like *as well as, in spite of, with regard to*.

2. The form and meaning conveyed by the preposition is usually different in the student's language; therefore, English prepositions are difficult to translate and learn.

3. A change in preposition can change meaning.

   ▶ Was Tom *at the zoo*? or Was Tom *in the zoo*?

4. When prepositions are bound to certain noun, verb, or adjective meanings, ESL students have problems remembering to insert the preposition.

▶ I am interested biology class.

In the above sentence, ESL writers may omit the *in* that is bound to *interested*.

5. One preposition, like *in*, can have a variety of meanings as shown in the table below.

Examples	Meaning
His pen is *in his pocket*.	location
His vacation is *in June*.	time
In his class, there are thirty-four students.	membership of a group
He likes to ski *in the snow*.	during a type of weather
The one hundred-year-old book is *in good condition*.	condition

Prepositions function to mark time, place, origin, destination, means, relation, and more. When using prepositions, ESL students must consider the meaning, function, and structure of the sentence. Even with consideration, ESL students make preposition errors: sometimes they use the wrong preposition; sometimes the preposition is omitted; and sometimes the preposition is added erroneously. The table below exemplifies these common errors.

Error	Example
wrong preposition	Bill has worked since ten years.
preposition added erroneously	What time does she leave off work?
omitted preposition	He is interested science.

Free and Bound Prepositions

Prepositions are classified as either free or bound prepositions. **Free prepositions** have meaning in themselves.

▶ I have her books *on* my bookshelf.

In the above sentence, the preposition *on* means touching and supported by. It is regarded as a preposition of location in this context. Other sentences also can use *on* by itself as a preposition of location. The meaning of *on* will be the same if the context is the same; therefore, the preposition *on* has meaning independent of the word to which it is attached. On the other hand, a **bound preposition** must be bound to another word to have meaning.

▶ Some ESL students *depend on* tutors for help.

In the above sentence, the verb *depend* must be linked to *on* for the preposition to have grammatical meaning.

▶ Some ESL students *depend* tutors for help.

Without the preposition *on* bound to the word *depend*, an ungrammatical sentence exists. These multiword units such as *depend on, listen to, back up* are known as phrasal verbs or prepositional verbs; ESL students must learn these as if they were one word. Also, multiword prepositional phrases such as *in spite of* contain bound prepositions. Chapter Three also contains information about prepositions.

As a way of review, the following chart classifies some of the kinds of prepositions.

Location	Direction	Time	Bound Prepositions
in	to	at	rely on
on	from	by	depend on
at	into	in	listen to
under	out of	on	look at

Practice 22: Prepositions—Free and Bound

In the following paragraphs, underline each of the preposition and classify each prepositions as either free or bound.

During the years 1892 to 1924 when immigrants arrived in the United States, many of them passed through Ellis Island. Because of its historical significance, today Ellis Island is a historical landmark and part of the Statue of Liberty National Monument. People are interested in their roots, so millions of visitors a year travel there to look at where their ancestors first got off a ship to see the land of freedom and opportunity. These ancestors saw the United States as a place to start over and to put down roots.

It wasn't until 1890 that Ellis Island was selected by the Federal government as the location for immigrants to enter the United States through the New York port. The immigration station formally opened on January 1, 1892. According to the official Ellis Island Web site, immigration was steady during the next few years and peaked in 1907 when, on a single day, 11,747 immigrants were processed on Ellis Island. Immigrants continued to arrive until 1924 when immigration started to drop off.[3]

Problems with Verbs

Often ESL students need help from tutors concerning verb grammar. Problems with the verb concepts of number, person, tense, aspect, modality, and mood usually persist in ESL students' writing. When you help ESL students with verbs in written essays or on assignments that focus exclusively on formation of particular verb forms, use ESL grammar books and textbooks which have excellent charts and graphic organizers to teach concepts central to English verb grammar.

Helping students: Try drawing a time line to help ESL students understand the particular verb tenses and aspects.

▶ I *have been studying* English since I began junior high school.

In this example, the verb is in the present perfect progressive. The action is in progress in the past, at present, and will probably continue in the future. Therefore, a timeline for the present perfect progressive would look like this:

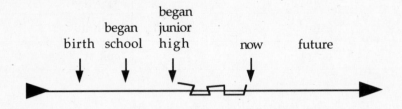

Auxiliary Verbs

As mentioned in Chapter Four, a verb fills the central position—the action or link— within the sentence. Verbs are distinguished as either auxiliary or main verbs. While many English classes use the term *helping verb*, ESL classes use the term *auxiliary verb*. Auxiliary verbs consist of the primary verbs *be, do,* and *have,* and a group of words known as modal auxiliary verbs: *can, could, may, might, will, would, shall, should,* and *must.*[1] Auxiliary verbs work in conjunction with main verbs and adverbs to express the concepts of time, aspect, modality, voice, mood, number, person, negation, and question formation. The following chart lists some of the auxiliary verbs.

DO	BE	HAVE	MODALS
does	am	has	can, could
do	is	have	may, might
did	are	had	will, would
	was		shall, should
	were		must

Modals

If you are a native speaker, you probably take modals for granted because native speakers express themselves naturally using modals. However, ESL students must learn why a certain modal is used in a particular situation to express a nuance of meaning. The following chart shows the meaning of the various modal auxiliaries.

Modal	Shows	Sentence Example
can, could	ability, possibility	Now that you no longer are sick, *can* you go surfing?
may, can, could	permission	You *may* have ice cream since you ate your dinner.
might, may	possibility	They *might* want to go fishing if there is no thunder and lighting tomorrow.
shall, will, would	to suggest or show intention	They *will* want to sell all the items to make the most profit.
should	advice or expectation	The singer *should* rest before completing her fast-paced concert tour.
must	obligation or necessity	The student *must* take the final exam.
would	intention, request, result, past habit	The administrators *would have* signed the cost of living agreement if the budget had been increased also.

Practice 23 Use of Modals

For each sentence below, choose the correct **modal**.

▶ You *might/may* take a raincoat with you just in case it rains.

1. He *could/should* have run faster if he had prepared for the marathon.
2. When you have finished cleaning your room, you *might/may* go to the movie.
3. Because of his health, he *could/should* give up the heavy responsibility.
4. In the morning, he *will/would* be leaving for the airport to get there early.
5. Because no one is seated after the play starts, we *must/shall* be on time tonight.
6. We knew that our team *would/must* win because the other team's star players were injured.

Subject-Verb Agreement

Both native and non-native English speakers have problems with subject-verb agreement. One technique that has proven to be useful in pointing out agreement errors to students is reducing the subject to its pronoun form and then asking for the verb form that agrees with the subject. For instance, consider the following error in agreement:

▶ *Monkeys* who live at a zoo where there is an open area *seems* to be happier.

Especially when there are intervening words between the subject and the verb, have the student look for only the subject and the main verb. Because the noun *monkeys* is plural, the student can substitute the plural pronoun *they* for the noun *monkeys* so that the student is focusing on the subject of the main clause.

▶ They *seems* to be happier.

Seems is the incorrect verb form because the verb must agree with the pronoun *they* and the plural noun *monkeys*.

Revised: They *seem* to be happier.

Therefore, the entire revised sentence should read:

Revised: *Monkeys* who live at a zoo where there is an open area *seem* to be happier.

Plagiarism in Student Writing

For more advanced ESL students, you may encounter tutoring sessions where students will be writing essays or research papers involving outside sources. In this context, you may find that a discussion of plagiarism is pertinent. Plagiarism is not as taboo in some other cultures as it is in the American culture. In the Chinese culture, using someone else's words is a compliment. Some cultures do not mark direct quotations and do not use citation systems such as the MLA or APA system. In your tutoring sessions, you can tactfully inform ESL students about signal phrases, quoting material, citing sources, paraphrasing, and summarizing. Along with their instructor teaching MLA or other citation methods, you can reinforce the teaching of these essential research writing skills in tutoring sessions.

Helping students: You will probably see research papers before instructors see them. If you suspect plagiarism, refrain from accusing students. Instead, remind them to summarize, paraphrase, or quote if they want to use the information that they have read. A tutorial session may be the first stage in acquainting students with a cultural value as well as an academic writing technique. If, within a paragraph, an idea appears to be from an expert and you suspect the idea is not the student's own, then ask the student if it was taken from a text which the student read. If so, explain how to introduce a source using a signal phrase within the text of the student paper.

Other Suggestions for Working with ESL Students

When tutoring ESL students, consider the following suggestions:

1. Greet and make students feel welcome. Get to know their names, and ask questions about their assignments. Many ESL students may feel uncomfortable or even scared. ESL classes are usually their first college classes, and students usually will seek out the writing center for help during their first semester, so put them at ease.

2. Keep tutoring sessions simple, and use easy-to-understand words.

3. It is essential to work with students' ESL textbooks as you conference with students so that they can see how to use their textbook as a reference.

4. When you review essays, focus on one, two, or three (at the most) types of errors in one session.

5. Refrain from looking at each successive error in an essay. First, read as much as necessary of an essay to determine the most prevalent type of error. Jot down that error type to start a list. Note the second and third type of error most frequently made. Then, work through the essay

addressing only the first error type. Explain to students the grammar concepts or punctuation rules, and allow students to correct all errors. Explain how you identified the error. For instance, if the most frequent error is verb tenses, go through the entire essay discussing the use of verb forms: number, person, tense, aspect, modality, voice, and agreement. Discuss why the verb form in a particular sentence needs to be corrected, or why the verb form in another sentence is already correct. Work on one grammar concept instead of overloading the student with too many grammatical principles in one tutorial session. If time permits, work through the essay reviewing the grammatical or mechanical concepts concerning the second and third most frequently made errors. Do not worry about finding and correcting all the errors. Engaging in tutoring sessions that focus on only certain error types does leave some errors remaining on the student's paper, but remember that tutors are teachers first; they are not editors. The job of a tutor is not to provide students with "A" papers, but to help students learn writing and grammar concepts and to put these concepts into practice as they write.

6. Use ESL dictionaries. These dictionaries, such as the *The American Heritage English as a Second Language Dictionary* or *The Longman Advanced American Dictionary*, provide specific information for ESL students that is not provided in a dictionary written for native speakers of English. ESL students need to expand their vocabulary. However, refrain from making word choices for ESL students. Ask them the idea they specifically want to convey in a particular context; then they should use those words. Giving students a choice from a thesaurus or dictionary is better than giving words to students. When reading their students' papers, ESL instructors can spot words that are probably not part of their students' normal vocabulary.

7. When working with ESL students, you may feel compelled to work only on their sentence structure, word order, and word choice problems. What about helping with the content area of their essays? If you are working with a more advanced ESL writer, will you be able to allow time to focus on thesis statements, organization, coherence, transitions, and other areas of content? The answer should be *yes*.

    Most essays by ESL students will contain language problems that result in awkward word choice or wrong word forms as well as problematic phrase, clause, and sentence structure. These problems taken together may make comprehension of the paper difficult. In such cases, you cannot ignore these basic usage problems. Before discussing the thesis statement, you, as well as any other person reading the essay, must understand the sentences being written. You will probably have to first address the grammar and word choice problems so that the writing can be understood. To be fair to the ESL student, addressing the content and organization of any essay should also be part of the conference.

8. Avoid writing for ESL students. Giving students the words and sentences is not going to help them learn how to write sentences in English. Instead,

discuss the topic. Encourage students to verbalize the thoughts they are trying to express. Synthesize their thoughts into the simplest form after you listen to what the student says. If students are having trouble formulating sentences, identify the subject and verb, and then encourage students to add the details. Remind students how to connect words or ideas correctly to add support to their general statements.

9. Most current editions of grammar handbooks have a special ESL section covering areas of grammar with which ESL students often have problems. Be sure to read those sections in several different handbooks.

10. Your center's director might ask ESL instructors to lead workshops covering areas that are especially problematic for tutors to explain. Attend these workshops, if given, or talk to ESL instructors one-on-one. ESL instructors work with ESL students everyday, and these instructors can provide great insight.

Section III

Constructing the Edifice: Helping Students with Essays and Research Papers

Chapter 9

The Writing Process and Defining Audience and Purpose

"I want you to help me fix this essay," the student announces as he slides a typed document across the tutoring table.

You ask a few probing questions, glance at the document and may discover that

- the student has almost completed the essay and needs some organizational hints
- the essay lacks a clear focus
- the essay's thesis statement seems weak or is missing entirely
- the essay lacks well-developed main points and related support
- the essential steps of determining the audience and purpose of writing through some form of prewriting have been skipped altogether or are so loosely defined that the paper lacks any direction whatsoever

Where do you start? If the student's essay generated problems like those listed above and the sentences in the student's essay are reasonably sound, then start by helping the student define his or her audience and purpose and by assisting the student to organize and to focus the content of the essay. Worry about the sentence level fine-tuning once the essay is complete and coherent.

Writing an essay is much like constructing a building. Constructing a substantial foundation will allow the builder to assemble a strong frame which, in turn, will lead to a well-built building. In the same way, when constructing an essay, strong sentences lead to substantial paragraphs that form together to make a well-written essay. Chapters Three through Eight focused on sentence level issues so that a strong foundation could be laid. Now, beginning in Chapter Nine, the focus will be on building the edifice itself— that is, on exploring methods to help students through the writing process from defining audience and purpose to completing that final draft. Therefore, to begin this building process, Chapter Nine will discuss the writing process in general and then take a more detailed look at the first step in writing: defining audience and purpose

The Writing Process

As a tutor, you must have a clear view of the writing process and how each part or segment is interwoven to produce a clear, well-unified piece of communication. A tutor does not merely "correct" an essay; rather a tutor critiques a piece of communication designed to present a subject for thoughtful consideration and analysis by the reader. In brief, the writing process includes:

1. **Defining audience and purpose**. Writers must have an audience to whom they can address the writing, and they must also have some purpose in mind to construct an essay with well-defined main points and support. If students write without first thinking about the audience or the purpose, the result is an unfocused essay full of broad generalizations.

2. **Pre-writing and exploring**. The objective of pre-writing is to develop a working thesis and generate the main points of an essay. Pre-writing includes, but is not limited to, brainstorming, clustering, listing, questioning, freewriting, outlining, and "zero draft" writing.[1] Zero draft writing is writing a complete essay beginning to end in a short period of time and then extracting thesis and organizational structure from the essay paragraphs. As are all the forms of pre-writing, zero draft will be discussed more fully later on.

    The act of writing is an exciting process of *discovery*. Therefore, the purpose of the pre-writing stage is to discover a thesis that will be narrow enough and also to generate main points that will be specific enough to facilitate getting started. Yet, pre-writing has other uses than just helping the writer get started. Once the writing of the first draft has begun, a writer can also use these "pre-writing" techniques at any time to refine the thesis, to develop main points, and to discover new insights, examples, and details.

3. **Writing a first draft**. In writing first drafts, writers seek to breathe life into their ideas. Pre-writing helps capture ideas. Pre-writing can even capture a writer's feeling and emotions, but it does not necessarily bring those ideas to life for the reader. That is, pre-writing helps the writer organize his thoughts, but pre-writing does not, as a rule, fully develop those ideas, feelings, or impressions into a form that can touch a reader's senses, provoke a reader's thoughts, or show relationships between ideas. For a writer to touch a reader's senses, the writer must translate the ideas captured during the pre-writing into fully developed sentences and paragraphs that contain specific support and concrete detail. Through this process of creating a first draft, the writer will link crucial

thoughts that will ultimately be molded into a well-developed essay or longer work. In fact, the mere process of placing sentences and paragraphs in a specific order will force a writer to think more deeply about the ideas generated in the pre-writing stage. Yet, writing the first draft is not the end of the process because the ideas need to be clarified and refined through editing and revising.

4. **Editing and revising the draft from an organizational point of view**. During editing and revising stages, writers critically analyze and examine their essays to be sure the writing succinctly states the intended purpose and to be sure that the issues discussed suit the intended audience. During the revision process students can

- examine the thesis to be sure that it is not too narrow nor too broad
- change or adjust the thesis if the drafting process has resulted in a change in focus or view
- strengthen main points
- clarify (or perhaps more clearly develop) support to include specific and concrete details, examples, and illustrations
- sharpen commentary and discussion
- unify introduction, body, and conclusion

Peer critique is an important step in essay revision, and you, as tutor, are providing that step.

Helping students: While reviewing an essay, do not hesitate to have the student read it aloud or you might read it to the student. Reading aloud will help the student hear the flow of his or her essay as well as detect errors in logic and organization.

5. **Producing a final draft.** At this stage, pay particular attention to the grammar and mechanics using a grammar handbook or other resource.

Students may ask for tutoring at any stage of the writing process. Ask questions to determine what steps students have taken and evaluate the essay to determine what steps need to be taken.

The operative word in understanding the way that people write is the word *process*. Writing creates a living, breathing entity that can trigger laughter, wrench out tears, and encourage thought and introspection. This process, though presented in the five above steps, is not linear. The process does not necessarily, nor is it required to, move step by step. The definition of audience and purpose and the experience of pre-writing will begin a process that revolves around drafting, revision; drafting, revision; drafting, revision and so on until a due date or deadline for submission brings an end to the process of writing (at least for the moment).

Defining Audience and Purpose

Perhaps the easiest way to discuss audience, purpose, and the writing process is to recreate a typical tutoring session so that you can see and hear tutoring in action. Through this fictional dialogue between you, the tutor, and a student tutee, you will gain insight into how to interact with students and how to encourage students to think more deeply about their writing. Assume that the instructor has assigned a persuasive essay addressing the topic:

> Laws holding parents responsible for the crimes of their children are (are not) unreasonable—why or why not?

Enter your student, who for the purpose of this dialogue will be named "Tutee." After you and Tutee sit down at a small table, you arrange your resource books so that Tutee's books, in addition to any notepads and papers, can be placed on the tutoring table. You politely greet Tutee, exchange names, and then ask how you can help.

TUTEE: I have an assignment for English 100; it's driving me nuts.

YOU: (*smile*) I think I can be of help. What is the assignment?

TUTEE: (*Tutee spreads out five hand-written pages with many crossed-out lines and then points to the statement on the assignment sheet: "Laws holding parents responsible for the crimes of their children are (are not) unreasonable—why or why not?" Tutee shrugs.*)

YOU: Ah, well . . . let's see. (*Here your gut feeling is to say, "Let's narrow the thesis," but then a little voice says, "What has the student done so far?"*) Yes, let's see what you've done so far. (*You shuffle papers.*) Do you know the purpose of your writing or do you have any idea of your audience?

TUTEE: (*momentary silence*) Well, the purpose is to get it done, and the audience is my teacher.

YOU: Okay . . . (*You glance at the papers and then look at Tutee.*) your instructor's prompt sounds like he or she wants you to take a position. What do you think?

TUTEE: Hmmmm.

YOU: If you know that your teacher wants you to take a position, then doesn't the purpose of the writing seem to be more than merely "to get the assignment done"? (*You lean back slightly, inviting an open response from Tutee.*)

TUTEE: Maybe.

YOU: (*Moments of silence pass, and with the feeling that this void must be filled, you repeat your question.*) Something more than merely "to get the assignment done"? (*"How can I encourage the student to dialogue with me?" you ask yourself.*)

TUTEE:	Of course. I am supposed to prove or show that laws holding parents responsible for the criminal acts of their children are either fair or unfair.
YOU:	(*Hallelujah! The student is responding—you try to remain stoic.*) Interesting words "prove or show." Are those terms that your instructor used?
TUTEE:	Yeah. I am supposed to prove or show and convince.
YOU:	Ah. "And convince"? Would it be safe to assume that the purpose of the paper is to convince the reader of your position?
TUTEE:	(*looks stunned*) Yeah.
YOU:	Well, whom do you plan to convince?
TUTEE:	The teacher.
YOU:	Good, but do you know your teacher well enough to tailor your convincing argument to fit his or her needs?
TUTEE:	I think so.
YOU:	Could you convince your brother, your close friend, or a neighbor more easily?
TUTEE:	Yes, but why? They don't care.
YOU:	Okay, but you should have the audience as specific as possible, one whom you know fairly well so that you can tailor your arguments to your audience's needs.

In brief, defining audience and establishing the purpose of writing are crucial steps to producing clear, concise, imaginative writing.

Helping students: Good techniques of tutoring involve asking leading questions to encourage students to think about their writing. Some questions to ask students to help them identify the audience and purpose include the following:

- What is a good reason for writing this paper?
- Are you aware that the purpose of a paper can be written or explained by using the word *to*? For instance, your purpose could be *to* explain, *to* convince, *to* classify, *to* compare, *to* contrast, *to* show cause, *to* show effect, *to* show both cause and effect, *to* tell a story, *to* describe, *to* tell how to do this or that, *to* argue (*to* prove logically) or *to* persuade (*to* touch the emotions with the intent of convincing).
- Is there any one person or any group who would benefit from knowing the information that you are providing in your essay?
- Do you know this person or group well enough to tailor specific, concrete details as well as arguments, examples, and illustrations that will help the reader see your point more clearly?
- Why should your topic appeal to your audience?
- Does the purpose of your essay clearly reflect the objective of the assignment? Be aware that the tutor's job is to help students with the basics of the writing process. This facilitation means that you must understand assignments to some degree. However, understanding assignments to help students write essays does not necessarily mean that you

must interpret assignments for them and do all the thinking for them. Students must determine the objective of their assignments because they are taking the classes while you, the tutor, are not taking those specific classes. You can ask questions to help students think more deeply about audience, purpose, and the thesis that is being addressed. If students, after brainstorming with you, still do not understand their assignments, perhaps you should suggest they conference with their instructors for further clarification or direction.

Chapter 10

Pre-writing Techniques and Outlining

Pre-writing is a valuable step that can facilitate critical reasoning and effective writing. Pre-writing, sometimes called "invention," includes

brainstorming	freewriting
clustering	zero draft writing
listing	outlining
questioning	

Producing Pre-writing

Many times students are in a hurry with their writing, so often they will skip the pre-writing step. If they address it at all, their concept is that pre-writing is merely a required step to be taken and that it falls within the boundaries of busy work. Therefore, if students have asked you to review completed essays, and you notice that the essays have organizational problems, be sure to check for evidence of pre-writing. If, on the other hand, students ask you for help in developing the essay, be sure to start with the pre-writing. Ideally, before you move to the development of a strong thesis and its related parts, you must encourage your tutees to explore what they already know about the subject. Pre-writing activities can help students discover the ideas and main points, as well as thesis and examples for their essays. These activities allow you, as tutor, to avoid the actual writing of the essay.

The basic rule for all pre-writing: Students should keep an open mind. The key to successful pre-writing is to withhold judgment and not reject any topic during the idea-generating stage. Sometimes the most bizarre or outlandish idea turns out to be the very element needed to set an essay well above the mundane. Remind students to let all ideas surface during pre-writing; they should record these ideas without comment or criticism. When every idea seems to have surfaced in the pre-writing step, then students may review their ideas, eliminating those that seem irrelevant or impractical.

As an illustration of helping with pre-writing, consider the following dialogue with another fictional tutee.

(Enter Tutee; assignment paper in hand. You move professionally through the preliminaries. Finally, the student suggests the reason for the visit.)

TUTEE:	I need help.
YOU:	Well, what is your assignment?
TUTEE:	*(pushes assignment paper in front of you and points)* This!
YOU:	*(read it quickly: "holding parents responsible . . ." You think, "I have just tutored a student addressing the same topic"; you slide the paper back to your new tutee.)* Have you written any notes down about your response to the topic?
TUTEE:	No. Not yet.
YOU:	What do you know about the subject? Is it fair to hold one person responsible for another person's actions?
TUTEE:	Maybe.
YOU:	Why maybe? Why not yes or no?
TUTEE:	It depends.
YOU:	Depends on what?
TUTEE:	Who the people are . . . like . . .
YOU:	Why does it depend on who the people . . . ?
TUTEE:	Like Cole.
YOU:	Who?
TUTEE:	Like my cousin Cole. He painted graffiti on a fence.
YOU:	What happened to Cole?
TUTEE:	Nothing. My aunt paid.
YOU:	Was that fair?
TUTEE:	What?
YOU:	That your aunt paid for an act that her son committed?
TUTEE:	I don't know. He's still doing it. Last week he painted graffiti on a building.
YOU:	Who paid this time?
TUTEE:	Cole was stupid. He should never have gotten caught.
YOU:	Did he have to pay?
TUTEE:	No. My aunt did. But, this is going nowhere. Are you going to help me or not?
YOU:	Of course! Actually, I think we are getting somewhere. Let's continue a few minutes longer on this line of thought.

Idea generation is tricky. First, the act of idea generation must be free and uninhibited. Second, it must be conscious and controlled. These two points seemingly contradict one another, yet to use idea generation effectively as a writing tool, the technique must include both of these elements. As a tutor, you need to help students work through one or more idea-generation techniques even when students have lost focus or do not grasp the assignment. Always keep in mind that most idea generators can be used at anytime during the writing process to help generate initial ideas, to refine a supporting point or the thesis, to generate and amplify examples and illustrations, or merely to help focus the essay in general.

The Pre-Writing Tools at Your Disposal

Brainstorming. This technique involves thinking and generating ideas and writing them down.

> **Helping students:** You can best use brainstorming with students by pulling out a blank piece of paper (8 $1/2$ x 11 preferably) and asking them to write as many ideas about the subject as they can. Although, in most instances, tutors should let students do all their own writing, here you may want to assist students by recording their exact words. Start by recording the general topic in the middle of the page, and then sprinkle the ideas around this general topic. As you record their ideas, place them randomly on the page—do not stack one on top of the other as if you are listing, and do not number these ideas. Brainstorming is a random collecting of ideas, and this exercise should visually reflect this idea. Record everything; leave out nothing that students say out loud (no matter how inappropriate or bizarre it seems). From this brainstorming exercise, students can cull potential main points, illustrations, and examples and then later organize them into a working outline.

Clustering. This technique groups brainstorming ideas into similar topics.

> **Helping students:** To create a cluster, as students think of ideas, they should

- place the general topic at the center of the page and circle that topic
- brainstorm ideas so that the page looks like bits of a puzzle strewn across the table
- begin to look for common threads or ideas
- circle the common ideas and connect them with a line to other similar ideas

> For instance, if you were tutoring a student writing on the topic "significant events in my life," the student should write that topic in the center of the page and circle it. Next, you and the student should brainstorm about the topic. When brainstorming ideas about significant events in one's life, the ideas of first kiss, first date, first marriage, baby's first step, first day of school, first day at college,

and first child might appear, and they all have a common element of "first."

Next, the "firsts" are circled and connected with a line to the main topic and then connected to all the other "firsts" (see an example of clustering below). Ultimately, students will create a spider's web of connected ideas that indicate possible main and subordinate points. Students are now in a position to develop the idea of "firsts" by focusing on each supporting point and then adding any additional ideas that will provide more specific, concrete facts and examples.

Example of Clustering

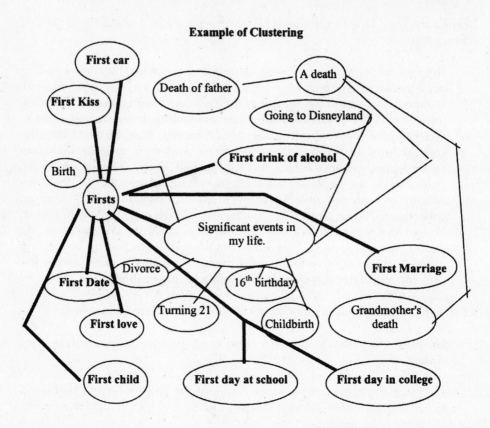

Listing. Listing is a means of generating ideas. Similar to brainstorming, in this pre-writing activity, students record ideas in a single column. Once students have run out of ideas, they can then reorganize their lists to group similar items together and to prioritize those ideas into main and subordinate points. A list focusing on "first experiences" might look like the following.

Firsts
1. First date
2. First child
3. First day of school
4. First day in college
5. First marriage
6. First kiss
7. First drink of alcohol
8. First love
9. First car

Listing is a powerful tool, but it has one pitfall—it implies a priority. The mere act of listing implies that the most important item or idea is going to be #1. To use listing effectively in the pre-writing stage, remind students to look beyond item #1 and to treat all ideas on the list as being equally important—any one of the items on the list could make a fine topic.

Questioning. Questioning is applying the journalist's questions to a topic. Questioning can be used in brainstorming and listing to generate new ideas or help develop the ideas already generated.

> **Helping students:** In brief, you need to ask students: who, what, where, when, why, and how. As an example, return to the previous section's fictional tutoring session about holding parents responsible. Recall that the tutor asked questions such as "Was that fair?" which is another form of "why." In the essay prompt about holding parents responsible for the acts of their children, you could ask students the following questions:
>
> - At what age do children become responsible for their own actions?
> - When is holding the parents responsible "fair"?
> - When is holding the parents responsible "unfair"?
> - What specific circumstances make holding the parents responsible fair or unfair?
> - Who would benefit by holding parents responsible for the actions of their children?
> - What would the child learn? What would the parents learn?

Freewriting. Freewriting puts idea generation in motion. Students can use freewriting to discover a topic or subject, or they can use freewriting to explore a given topic. It simulates writing the essay in that freewriting uses complete sentences and paragraphs to capture the ideas generated.

Helping students: To freewrite, merely set a timer for five or ten minutes, and then ask students to write as much as they can. During freewriting, they should

- disregard all grammar, mechanics, and spelling rules
- continue writing, non-stop, for five to ten minutes. If students cannot think of anything to write, they need to write over and over "I can't think of anything to write."

The idea is to capture spontaneous, free-flowing ideas, so do not allow students to stop to repair spelling errors, comma placement, or re-collect their thoughts. Their fingers should keep clicking that keyboard or pushing that pen so that constant writing is sustained until the time period is completed. When the period has concluded, the writing produced may or may not read like an essay. You can help students by having them highlight the ideas that surfaced in the freewriting text. Then show students how to reorganize these ideas into a list or outline for the eventual essay.

Zero draft writing. In zero draft writing, writers need not use other forms of pre-writing (but pre-writing would help); writers merely need to have a feel for the central idea they want to discuss and, perhaps, an idea about how the essay might begin or end. The basic idea of zero draft writing is to generate a complete essay with an introduction, body, and conclusion as well as to produce it in a short period of time, for instance in a single sitting if possible. Writers should be as specific as possible, but they should also resist the urge to pause or to go back to add details; they need to keep pushing through to the end. Once the zero draft essay is complete, writers can begin to edit and to reorganize.

Helping students: After students have completed a zero draft, you can be of help. While refraining from being an editor or proofreader, help students extract outlines, help students to identify more clearly the central ideas they are trying to prove or show, or ask questions to help define the main points, specific details, examples, and conclusion. Though students may despair at the many changes, remind students that zero drafts are written to be edited, rearranged, and massaged into a real essay. Sometimes only a few supporting points in the zero draft are actually retained while the rest of the supporting points are thrown out; other times, many of the sentences in a zero draft need little more than minor revisions. Also, unlike a freewriting that can be done during a tutoring session, zero draft writing should be completed outside of the tutoring session.

Outlining. Depending on the stage in the writing process and personal preference, writers will use either a formal or informal outline to help manage the essay.

- **The formal outline** reflects the supporting main points, examples, illustrations, and discussion that will be used to prove the thesis. Since the formal outline usually reflects the arrangement of the final draft of the essay, the formal outline is often written after the essay is complete. When conferencing with students in the initial stages of writing an essay, the formal outline is not used as a pre-writing activity because it demands a tremendous amount of specific, concrete detail and because its structure is too restrictive for preliminary stages of writing. On the other hand, a formal outline provides an excellent organizational tool once the writing of the essay is well underway.

- **The informal outline** lists the proposed thesis and supporting main points. It provides supportive detail in a more general sense than the formal outline. In addition, the informal outline's form is also less restrictive than that of the formal outline. It also explores the depth and detail of the supporting points more fully than a mere list.

Helping students: Because the formal outline is usually written after the essay is complete, you should work primarily with the informal outline. As you have done with the other forms of pre-writing, begin by asking students pertinent questions to help generate possible main points, supportive details, and a potential thesis. Once students have a tentative thesis in mind or even an idea that they want to prove or show, the informal outline can be used to help generate supporting main points, specific details, and examples. After the informal outline is constructed, it can be used to explore supporting main points in relationship to the thesis and then used to modify the thesis or the supporting main points. To create the informal outline, begin with the thesis statement—the central idea that students want to show or prove. Then, beneath the thesis statement, students need to list the main points that show or prove that thesis. As students generate outlines, ask them the following questions:

- What supporting main points will probably show or prove the thesis?
- Do these main points actually show or prove the thesis? Why or why not?
- How can each main point be stated so that the relationship between the main points and the thesis is clearly indicated?
- What specific details, examples, or illustrations can be added so that the reader can clearly "see" or understand each supporting main point?
- What is the most important point that the essay will emphasize in the conclusion?

Though the answers to these questions can be written in short phrases or fragments, students should use complete sentences in fleshing out the main points and support. The basic outline format could look something like the following sample outline.

Thesis Statement: Write the main point—the central idea—that the essay will show or prove. This statement could be one sentence or several sentences, depending on the expected length of the essay.

1. **First main point** to show or prove the thesis
   a. Support and discussion to show or prove first main point
   b. Example to show or prove first main point
   c. Commentary that ties the example to the first main point and the first main point to thesis

2. **Second main point** to show or prove thesis
   a. Support and discussion to show or prove second main point
   b. Example to show or prove second main point
   c. Commentary that ties the example to the second main point and the second main point to thesis

3. **Third and additional main points** (follow above format)

Conclusion: Rephrase the central idea of the essay and stress its importance.

To use the outline as an effective tool, think of the outline as an entity that is flexible and subject to change. The outline begins in a rough or scratch form and may reflect only a loosely defined thesis and a few supporting main points. As the writer ponders the thesis and ways to show or prove it, the thesis and main points become more specific; then, possible facts, concrete details, discussion, and examples are added to the outline of the essay. This expanded informal outline now provides sufficient information and will serve as a basis for the student to begin writing the essay and to help the student control the logical flow of ideas and support.

Continuing with the suggested topic of holding parents responsible for the crimes of their children, the student may have written an informal outline similar to the one below with place holders *example needed here* to indicate examples that the writer must still provide.

Central Idea: Holding parents responsible for the criminal acts of their teenage children is unfair.

Thesis: Though the legislature is considering enacting laws that hold parents both financially and morally responsible for their children's criminal actions, a law that would hold parents responsible for the criminal acts of their teenagers who are sixteen to eighteen years old would be an injustice to the parents and a disservice to the teen and to the community.

1. **Introduction:** Individuals must, at some point in their lives, become accountable for their own actions. This point of taking responsibility

begins when teenagers accept their drivers' licenses and the responsibilities that accompany driving.

2. Driving a car requires mature thinking and the ability to respond to life-threatening situations.

   a. Example or illustration needed here.

   b. If teens can take the responsibility of driving, then they have the capability to determine right from wrong.

3. Sixteen- to eighteen-year-olds are almost adults and often think and act like adults.

   a. Need example, illustration, or more clarification here.

   b. Teenagers who drive have the capacity and often demand the right to be treated as adults.

   c. Discussion: why would the courts treat these "adults" as children?

4. Many sixteen- to eighteen-year-old people are fathers and mothers, working full time.

   a. They are no longer under the control of parents.

   b. Need example here.

   c. Why should parents be held liable for the actions of these "adult" children whether the children are married or not?

5. Parents can control the actions of small children, but teens can and do think for themselves.

   a. Need example and more discussion here.

   b. These teens, ages sixteen to eighteen, need to take full responsibility for their own actions, and this responsibility includes accepting the consequences of committing a criminal act.

6. Holding parents responsible for the crime of their sixteen- to eighteen-year-old teens only encourages teens to commit other crimes because laws exact no penalty on teens.

   a. Need specific, concrete details.

   b. Need example and discussion here.

Conclusion: Therefore, laws that hold parents accountable for the actions of their teenage children sixteen to eighteen years of age would be an injustice to the parents and the teenager. If a teenager can take the responsibility of driving a car, he or she can assume the responsibility for his or her own actions.

In this informal outline, the student needs to refine the support and provide sufficient details, examples, and illustrations. With this scratch outline, the student can now create an essay.

Helping students with pre-writing in general: You do not have to insist that students go through any of the pre-writing techniques listed above. However, should you sense that students have not done sufficient thinking about the topic, you might take them through one or more of the pre-writing techniques. Since you should avoid writing for students or writing directly on their essays, and since you are to conduct tutoring sessions orally, the most useful pre-writing tools for you to use include questioning, brainstorming, clustering, or listing. Remember that your function is to stimulate the ideas by asking pertinent questions while the students' responsibility is to do the thinking, the organizing, and the writing.

Chapter 11

Thesis, Body, Support, Introduction, and Conclusion

Once students have concluded the pre-writing, they are ready to move on to developing the full essay. In this chapter, you will look at those elements that constitute a well-developed and well-organized essay:

- thesis statement
- body paragraphs and support of the thesis statement
- development of the supporting main points
- development of body paragraphs
- use of transitions
- formulating the introduction and conclusion

Formulating the Thesis Statement

Formulating a thesis statement can sometimes be best understood as it unfolds in the action itself. The example discussed in the outlining section in the previous chapter assumed that the tutee had developed a thesis; however, the actual development of that thesis can be a task in itself. Therefore, consider the tutee who has not clearly defined or developed his or her thesis. This assumption will allow you to observe how a thesis is formulated as Chapter Ten's fictional tutoring session picks up with you and Tutee using cousin Cole as an example.

YOU: Who paid this time?
TUTEE: My aunt. But this is going nowhere. Are you going to help me or not?
YOU: Yes, of course! Doesn't it seem a bit unfair that your aunt paid for damage that Cole created?
TUTEE: (*Tutee ponders the question a moment.*) Well, I guess so.
YOU: Nevertheless, did it seem unfair that nothing happened to Cole?

113

TUTEE: (*Tutee rustles papers anxiously.*) How does this get my paper
            written?
YOU: Your selected topic is what?
TUTEE: Whether holding parents responsible for their children's crimes is
            fair or unfair.
YOU: So, you need to select a side, a position. Is it fair or unfair? Think
            of your aunt and Cole. Do you think you could use Cole's situation
            as an example to show your position?
TUTEE: Well, it seems fair. Something should have happened . . . Oh, I
            could write: "Holding parents responsible is fair." I mean, no way
            could Cole have ever paid for the mess he created.
YOU: True. But is it fair always, in all cases?
TUTEE: Why isn't it?
YOU: You said Cole committed the vandalism while his parents picked
            up the tab. Should Cole have paid something?
TUTEE: I guess so. It really ticked me off . . .
YOU: Then you think it is unfair that the parents paid?
TUTEE: No. Cole needed to help pay, and besides his parents should have
            brought him up better; that's what my mom says.
YOU: What if Cole assaulted someone? Should Mom and Dad be held
            responsible then?
TUTEE: No. Well, if Cole had been little, I mean seven or eight . . . maybe
            twelve, but . . .
YOU: So, age has something to do with whether the parent or the child
            holds responsibility? Then, is Cole too young to be held
            responsible?
TUTEE: He can drive a car; can't he?
YOU: He has his license? Does driving a car have something to do with
            being responsible?
TUTEE: Well . . . I guess Cole should have paid.
YOU: You don't sound too sure. Can you take a side? Is Cole responsible or
            his parents? Can you formulate a thesis about one side that you
            can show or prove?
TUTEE: Oh. Do you mean a thesis like "Holding parents responsible for
            the crimes of their children is fair when the children are less
            than sixteen"?
YOU: You have the idea.
TUTEE: I mean, if the child is responsible enough to drive a car, shouldn't
            that child be old enough to take responsibility for his or her
            actions?
YOU: Now you are getting somewhere.

    To narrow the thesis, writers should focus on the central idea that they
are trying to prove or show, the main points necessary to prove that central
idea, the audience, the purpose, and the scope of the writing. The length or
scope of the thesis will vary according to these elements. For instance, in the
above scenario, the student's first proposed "thesis" (holding parents respon-

sible is fair) was nothing more than the assignment prompt; as a result, the scope was far too large for an assignment of five hundred to one thousand words (two to four typewritten pages). As you deal with students, remember that most teachers expect their students to limit the thesis of the essay—in short, limiting the thesis is required as part of the assignment. If students merely restate prompts, their essays will not show individual thinking, nor will their essays present fully developed ideas and new thoughts.

A good thesis presents an opinion or judgment, as well as suggests a specific direction for the essay. The thesis will be the broadest statement in the essay. As a result, the thesis cannot be taken as either true or false without support provided by specific, concrete details in the form of main points, illustrations, examples, facts, and commentary or discussion. These elements, working together, will show or prove the thesis to be true.

Again, consider Tutee's first thesis statement: "Holding parents responsible is fair." As stated, the thesis sounds adequate, yet it is too broad because the thesis creates too many questions that must be answered. This thesis is not entirely useless, for it would make a good working thesis for an initial pre-writing activity or even a first draft. However, as a student attempts to show or prove this particular thesis, he or she would find the essay growing larger and larger. In theory, a writer, at some point, should recognize that the scope is too large. Yet, most student writers often miss this point and plunge right into the writing of their essays using the "working thesis" without change. You can help students explore the possibilities and then encourage students to create a thesis that can fit the purpose of their assignments and can be fully discussed in the body of the paper.

Helping students: To ascertain whether a given sentence is an appropriate sentence for a thesis statement, you and the student writer should look at the student's thesis statement, and you might ask the following questions:

- Does this thesis sentence contain an opinion or judgment and give the reader direction?
- Does this sentence seem too broad or too narrow, thus lacking clear direction and a specific, clearly stated opinion or judgment?
- Does this sentence suggest an expected length of an essay?
- Does the suggested scope of this sentence fit the assignment; how many words or pages would it take to develop the opinion or judgment suggested in the sentence?

Remember that developing a thesis statement can often require several sentences or paragraphs if the essay is long, or the thesis may be implied but not captured in a given sentence. Therefore, look at the entire essay. In general, encourage basic level students to include a thesis; for a more advanced writer, work toward presenting a clear position or central idea.

Practice 24 Analyzing Thesis Statements

Using the above questions as a guide, explain why each of the following sentences would or would not make a good thesis statement.

1. The movie *Shakespeare in Love* is nice.
2. The movie *The Lord of the Rings: The Fellowship of the Ring* demonstrates a greater degree of artistic directing than did the movie *Harry Potter and the Sorcerer's Stone*.
3. The death of Nanapush, in Louise Erdrich's *The Last Report on the Miracles at Little No Horse*, demonstrates the humor of the character Nanapush and the humor of the author.
4. Morgan le Fey, in Marion Zimmerman Bradley's *Mists of Avalon*, exerts her power as a woman by refusing to take a subservient role to men as dictated by social customs of King Arthur's day.
5. The Lady of the Lake saved King Arthur's life on more than one occasion.
6. According to Bruce Catton's essay "Grant and Lee," General Robert E. Lee surrendered to General U.S. Grant at Appomattox Courthouse, April 9, 1865.
7. Robert E. Lee can most assuredly be called a "Tidewater Aristocrat."
8. New York City was attacked on September 11, 2001.
9. When the rhyme and rhythm become the dominant elements of a poem, the poem's meaning is lost in the hum and thump of the sound of language.
10. William Carlos Williams, in his poem "Dedication for a Plot of Ground," dramatically demonstrates the power of repetition as an effective tool to drive home the poem's meaning.

Body Paragraphs and Support of Thesis Statement

At this point, most textbooks would move into a discussion of developing strong body paragraphs to support the thesis. However, as a tutor, you are often given a "completed" essay, so in looking at a student's organization and structure, you must analyze both the thesis and the body concurrently. Therefore, you need to understand the role of the thesis and supporting points to help the student understand how to produce strong, well-developed points.

Helping students: In revising completed essays, students should either:

- add, delete, or modify the main points and related support to clearly show or prove the thesis, or
- change or modify the central idea of the thesis to adequately include existing main points and related support.

Look at the student's essay as a unit and ask the simple question: What does the writer want to prove or show? To answer this question effectively, you must discover the purpose of the student's writing, the question being answered by the student's essay.

Before setting out on one of these avenues—helping the student adjust the main points to fit the thesis or shape the thesis to fit the main points—you need to be familiar with the assignment or objective of the writing. However, do not interpret the assignment for the student; rather, let the student interpret the assignment for you. Then, determine whether the paper sufficiently addresses the assignment as explained by the student. Since you are not taking that class, not attending the lectures, nor reading the textbooks, the student, not you, should make the final determination whether the essay fulfills the requirements of the assignment.

Once you understand the assignment in general, read the paper, and then discuss with the student which of the two avenues of departure best fit the essay.

Regarding thesis: In addition to ascertaining if a thesis statement presents an opinion or judgment, you might ask the student the following questions:

- What central idea is this essay trying to prove or show?
- Can you identify one sentence or a group of sentences that expresses the central idea that the essay is claiming to prove or show? Though instances exist when no stated thesis can be found in an essay, most college writing usually demands that a specific thesis be presented. The thesis, in effect, constitutes the answer to the writing prompt in general, while the body and support paragraphs provide the reasons why the thesis is true.
- Based on the thesis statement, what type of support do you expect to see in the body?

Regarding the support: As you discuss an essay's supporting paragraphs, you might ask the student these questions:

- What are the main points of the essay?
- Do the main points directly show or prove the thesis?
- If the main points do not seem to relate to the thesis as identified, what thesis statement do these points support? (*Hint:* look for key words or phrases that may be repeated.)
- Is each main point clearly supported by specific, concrete facts and details?
- Is each main point supported by a clear and relevant example or illustration?
- Does commentary or discussion link the specific details, examples, and illustrations to the main point?

What Constitutes Good Development?

Every essay in some way follows the developmental pattern of an introduction, body, and conclusion. When these parts are organized, unified, and coherent, the essay shines; it produces the feeling of completeness. In the well-written essay, the main points clearly support the thesis, the thesis is appropriate for the audience and purpose, and the conclusion gives the reader a feeling that the essay has ended.

Focusing on the supporting main points (that is, the body paragraphs of the essay), the writer must provide at least one, fully developed paragraph for each supporting main point of the essay but could, and should, use more paragraphs for each point when the topic demands. However, what constitutes a well-organized and developed paragraph? In brief, a well-written body paragraph should contain these elements:

- a topic sentence that expresses the controlling idea—an opinion or judgment that needs to be shown or proven
- facts and details—the supporting points that prove or show the topic sentence
- examples and illustrations in specific, concrete detail that show or prove this point
- commentary or discussion that explains how the examples or illustrations show the supporting points and how these two elements together show or prove the topic sentence
- commentary or discussion that explains how the entire paragraph shows or proves the thesis statement

Though like a thesis statement, topic sentences can be implied but not stated directly, most paragraphs usually contain a topic sentence that will express the main point of the given paragraphs and contain sufficient concrete details and information to allow the reader to see clearly the point being made. Also, every paragraph must relate to (prove or show) the thesis statement (the central idea of the essay) either directly or indirectly.

The basic structure used for developing the entire essay and the basic structure used for developing a strong, well-unified paragraph are similar. More specifically, each paragraph in an essay is like a little essay in itself; each paragraph contains a central or controlling idea to be proven or shown, to be explained, and thus, to be fully developed. The following table shows the similarity between the development of an entire essay and the development of one body paragraph.

DEVELOPMENT OF THE ESSAY'S CENTRAL IDEA	DEVELOPMENT OF THE TYPICAL BODY PARAGRAPH
For Each Supporting Main Point (in one or more paragraphs)	**Topic Sentence**
1. Facts, details, and supportive points 2. Examples and illustration 3. Commentary to explain how examples prove or show main point 4. Commentary or discussion to explain how main point and its related illustrations and examples prove or show the thesis statement 5. Conclusion	1. Facts, details, and supportive points 2. Examples and illustration 3. Commentary to explain how examples prove or show facts, details, and supportive points 4. Commentary or discussion to explain how the topic sentence and examples prove or show the relationship of the paragraph to the rest of the paper 5. Conclusion and/or transition to next paragraph

Use of Transitions

Transitions are used to link the idea of one paragraph to the idea of another paragraph and to link the idea of one sentence to the idea of another sentence. They are powerful tools that improve the coherence and unity of a paragraph and facilitate the flow of ideas from one sentence or paragraph to the next. To help students use transitions within their essays, think of an essay as a series of boxes that present main points, specific details, explanations, and examples. These boxes are linked together with transitions, so between the boxes students should write the sentence(s) that help readers move from one paragraph or main point to the next.

Helping students: To use this technique, have students outline their essays. Enclose the essay elements (the introductory points, each of the body points with its support, and the conclusion) in their own separate boxes, and ask students to write transitional sentence(s) that will help readers link the idea of one paragraph to the idea of the next paragraph as shown in the following diagram.

```
+----------------------------+
|   Introductory             |
|   Paragraph                |
+----------------------------+
```

Transitional Sentence

```
+----------------------------+
|   Body Paragraph           |
|   Main point, support,     |
|   examples                 |
+----------------------------+
```

Transitional Sentence

```
+----------------------------+
|   Body Paragraph           |
|   Main point, support,     |
|   examples                 |
+----------------------------+
```

Transitional Sentence

```
+----------------------------+
|   Concluding               |
|   Paragraph                |
+----------------------------+
```

A variation of the box technique is to think of each paragraph in a circle with each transition in an interconnecting circle that overlaps the previous paragraph's circle and next paragraph's circle. In this way the transition is providing unity between those two paragraphs.

Transitions can link more than paragraphs; transitional words or phrases can link sentences and parts of sentences such as phrases and clauses. Words such as *furthermore* and *for example* are examples of transitional words used to help the reader think through and logically link the ideas being presented as the reader moves sentence by sentence or paragraph by paragraph. However, transitions can also be paragraphs, complete sentences, subordinate or dependent clauses, or phrases as well as words. In short, transitions help create a coherent, well-unified paragraph or essay in which every element collaborates to create a clear focus.

Transitional words and phrases can be used to

- add an idea
- contrast an idea
- provide an alternative
- show similarity
- show order of time or order of idea
- show a result

- affirm
- give an example
- explain
- add an aside
- summarize

Guide students to use their own grammar handbook (or another writing center handbook) to locate appropriate transitional words or consult Chapter Three of this guide which lists the conjunctive adverbs or transitional expressions and provides you with examples.

Helping students: Transitioning between clauses, paragraphs, and even chapters helps readers maintain a logical flow of ideas. The lack of transitions can often produce choppy sentences; if the writing does not read smoothly, suggest that students use transitions as a means of linking one idea, one sentence, or one paragraph to the previous idea, sentence, or paragraph.

Introduction and Conclusion

At the beginning of the writing process, a working introduction is generally written to start the essay. However, since both the introduction and the conclusion need to reflect what will be or has been written in an essay, the actual sculpting and refining of these parts is usually saved until the organization and support is complete.

Introduction

When evaluating an introduction or conclusion, you will have the advantage of seeing the essay as a whole—as a complete unit. Therefore, before commenting too much on a student's introduction, be sure to read the entire essay or enough of the essay so that you understand the content and the point that the essay is trying to prove or show. Then, address the introduction using these questions:

- Is there a hook at the beginning of the essay that will pique the reader's attention and "reel the reader in" so that the reader will want to read the rest of the essay?
- Does the student discuss the topic in general before he or she narrows the thesis or before he or she moves to the body of the paper? (Remember that not all essays will have a thesis in the introduction, and some essays may not have a thesis at all.)
- Is sufficient background information given so that the reader can understand the topic that the essay will discuss?
- Is a direction for the essay suggested?
- Is a plan of organization suggested?
- If a plan of organization and development is suggested, does it follow the order presented in the body of the essay?
- Are key terms that are relevant to the discussion clearly defined?
- Is the tone established? The tone could be persuasive, informative, serious, humorous, personal, impersonal, formal, or informal.
- Is the thesis clearly stated?

Helping students: Introductions are meant to catch the reader's attention and generate an interest in the topic. However, the type of essay written or the type of assignment given may preclude a thesis statement in the introductory section. Therefore, look for the thesis, but do not insist that the introduction contain a thesis statement. Also, the above questions are meant to help analyze an essay's introduction. However, not all of the elements implied by these questions may be present—and you may discover other elements that are not listed above. An introduction is meant to introduce the general subject area in a lively and interesting fashion.

Conclusion

The job of the conclusion is to end the essay in such a way that the reader feels he or she has finished reading the essay. Every conclusion should remind the reader of the central idea that the essay is trying to prove or show. However, mirroring the central idea of the essay is not the only objective of a conclusion. Students can close an essay using other methods including the following:

- reminding the reader of the main point addressed in the essay
- projecting into the future, based on concrete facts discussed in the body of the essay
- making suggestions for possible solutions to a problem posed in the essay
- discussing the significance of the topic in relation to the position taken in the essay
- ending with an event, a narrated story, a hook, or a symbol initiated in the introduction
- using humor or a quote to tie the essay together

Two weaknesses that students often incorporate into the conclusion of their essays are stopping the discussion abruptly rather than drawing the discussion to a conclusion and introducing an entirely new topic, position, opinion, or twist on the thesis. As with other elements discussed in this guide, a lengthy presentation of introductions and conclusions can be found in many writing handbooks. Such a handbook should be the tutor's most often consulted reference, so it is prudent to keep one close at hand.

Chapter 12

Rhetorical Modes

While an introduction, thesis statement, topic sentences, body paragraphs with support, and a conclusion give organization to an essay, the use of various rhetorical modes gives structure to an essay. The rhetorical modes discussed in this chapter include:

- narration
- description
- exemplification
- definition

- process analysis
- classification and division
- comparison and contrast
- cause and effect

As writers organize their work, they should follow a logical plan of development. However, this structure should be "unseen"; the content and argument of an essay should always be the primary emphasis. The intent of this section is to list and briefly summarize each rhetorical mode.

Narration

Narration is telling a story or incident. Usually, though not always, narration is chronological—the writer is recounting a story from beginning to end. For example, if a young woman spends a wonderful evening with someone special and the next day she shares the evening's events with a close friend, she is narrating—telling a story. If a guy is driving home and his car is hit from the rear, when he tells the incident to the police officer and retells it to anyone else, he is narrating or telling a story. The key to narration is to place readers in the situation by appealing to their senses of seeing, hearing, tasting, touching, and smelling. Effective use of description is an important component of narration.

Description

Description is a powerful tool that allows the reader to become part of the writing. Description involves using specific, concrete details to allow the reader to taste, touch, smell, hear, see, or feel emotion. George Simpson, for example, used description to hook the reader in his *New York Magazine* article "The War Room at Bellevue":

> Bellevue. The name conjures up images of an indoor war zone: the wounded and bleeding lining the halls, screaming for help while harried doctors in blood-stained smocks rush from stretcher to stretcher, fighting a losing battle against exhaustion and the crushing number of injured.[1]

Simpson uses words such as *bleeding, screaming, fighting* and *crushing* to place the reader in the emergency room. The use of these descriptive words helps the reader feel the pressure and stress that the nurses and doctors feel in Bellevue.

Exemplification, Facts, and Statistics

Exemplification simply means that the writer provides examples or illustrations through the use of specific, concrete details, relevant facts, and accurate statistics in such a way as to show the point or concept being discussed. For example, a student might want to talk about a creative sister, so the student writes: *My sister is very creative. For example, last year she won first prize in two new artists' contests.* Examples and illustrations can be short or extended; the length is not as important as the accurate showing of the point being made. Often certain transitional expressions such as *for example, such as, for instance, an illustration of,* or *in fact* introduce the example, illustration, facts, and statistics and help to create the logical link between the example and the point being shown or proven. Exemplification is used by all the other modes; as a result, many instructors do not consider exemplification a separate mode but rather consider it merely an essential part of the other modes.

Definition

Definition or the extended definition is more than quoting the definition provided by a dictionary because a dictionary definition does not provide sufficient depth or detail. The dictionary definition provides only the specific definition (called denotation) but does not convey the emotional or social nuances that are associated with a given word (called connotation). Often the term needing to be defined is an abstract term or concept that is crucial to proving the central idea or argument of an essay, so students need to use the extended definition mode as a means of providing a detailed explanation of the term. When students create the extended definition, they should use examples and illustrations, as well as other rhetorical modes (for example, compare and contrast or classification and division) to show both what the term *is*, as well as what the term *is not*.

Helping students: To help them understand the extended definition, suggest that students think of the difference between the concepts of *walk* and *stalk*. Both words, in a sense, mean to *walk*. However, to *walk* is neutral whereas to *stalk* carries more emotional and sociological connotation than does its dictionary definition of merely walking "stiffly, angrily, or haughtily."[2] Since most words have both a denotation and a connotation, you will find both native and non-native speaking students selecting words that do not quite fit the intended use.

For an example of an extended definition, ask students to consider this: if one defines *trust* as having a belief in something or someone, and one defines *belief* as having a trust in something or someone, then what is the difference, if any, between *belief* and *trust*? The best way to discern the difference is not to go to a dictionary and recite various meanings. Rather, students need to explain both *trust* and *belief* by showing each in action. For instance, consider this example:

> A high-wire act (performers who walk on tightropes) decided to run a tightrope across the Niagara River one mile from Niagara Falls. One tightrope walker wheeled an empty wheelbarrow across the tightrope over the river several times.
>
> When the performer was safely on the platform located on the Canadian side, he turned to a little boy in the audience. "Hop in. I'll give you a ride in my wheelbarrow," he said.
>
> "No way," said the boy.
>
> "Don't you believe I can take you across and back again safely?" asked the performer.
>
> "I believe you can," said the boy, "but I just don't trust you."

For this young person, a large divergence existed between *trust* and *belief*. *Belief* was an intellectual recognition that the act could be performed whereas *trust* required placing that belief into action. Extended definition, then, seeks to use examples, illustrations, and other rhetorical modes to help show the concept being defined.

Process Analysis

Process analysis is the how-to essay. When using process analysis, students are showing the how-to of something. In this rhetorical mode, the key organizational element is order of presentation. To skip a step or to provide a step out of order would derail the process, so each item explained must be presented in the order that the process dictates.

As an example, consider this situation: when a dad assembles a bicycle, he usually begins by laying out the all the necessary parts including front wheel, back wheel, handle bars, frame, pedals, front-wheel fork, and chain. For the dad, is the order of assembly important?

Yes. The dad needs to install the front-wheel fork (the part that the front wheel and the handle bars are attached to) before he can connect the front wheel to the bicycle frame. What about the back wheel to the frame? If he installs the back wheel before the chain, could he stretch the chain to go around the wheel sprockets? No, he cannot. He will need to loosen the back wheel, slide the chain over the sprocket, draw the back wheel back so that the chain is taut, and then tighten the back wheel. In essence, he needs to slide the back wheel into place after he has started putting the chain on. In other words, the back wheel and chain are installed simultaneously. So, order does matter, even when explaining how to assemble a bicycle. Anytime people are writing directions (explaining how to or explaining step-by-step), they are essentially writing a process analysis.

Helping students: Concerning point of view in essays, most instructors request that their students write in third person *he, she, it, one, they* because third person writing focuses on the subject being discussed. However, in process analysis, second person *you* is often the more preferable choice because it addresses the reader directly and makes the reader part of the essay. Also, when writing process analysis, the second person point of view creates a more friendly, informal tone whereas third person creates a formal, more wordy sentence structure. For instance, writing in second person, students might say, "first you attach the front-wheel fork to the bicycle frame, and then you attach the front wheel to the front-wheel fork." More directly, students might write (since in second person commands, the subject can be omitted): "attach the front-wheel fork to the frame, then attach the front wheel to the front-wheel fork." The same instructions in third person would read: "First one should attach the front-wheel fork to the bicycle frame. Then he or she should attach the front wheel to the front-wheel fork." Notice the extra words that are used and the formal or distant (uninvolved) tone that is created in third person. Therefore, many instructors recommend writing in second person when the writing assignment requires process analysis.

Helping ESL students: ESL instructors sometimes require that ESL students write a process essay in third person. In this exercise, even though the instructor is teaching the process mode, the instructor is also focusing on the proper use of modals (*would, should, could, may, must, might, can, will, shall*). The ESL instructor wants the student to write "one should . . ." rather than use the second person *you.*

Classification and Division

When explaining concepts, when showing cause or effect, or when comparing or contrasting, writers often need to group items into similar classes or divide items into smaller subdivisions so that readers can understand the writers' position. As students group or divide these items or concepts, they are employing the classification and division rhetorical mode. The key element in classification and division is to create a clearly defined line between each class or division. Though some overlap in classes often occurs, readers must understand where one class or division begins and ends and where the next class or division begins and ends. For example, the automobile constitutes one large class of vehicles separate from other vehicle types such as trucks. Additionally, automobiles can be divided according to different manufacturers—Ford, Chevrolet, Honda, Toyota—or can be divided according to types of vehicles based on use—sedan, sports car, truck, or SUV. The writer must clarify the classes or divisions using the purpose of writing and the audience as key components in making the distinction. Classification and division are powerful tools that assist other rhetorical modes such as compare and contrast.

Helping students: Students should list the classes and divisions so that they can better analyze the criteria being used to create the classes and divisions. This list would also help to organize the essay and ensure that the discussion order of the classes and divisions in the essay's body is the same order that is suggested in the introduction or pre-summary paragraph.

Compare and Contrast

When students compare and contrast two or more items or concepts, they are discussing the similarities and differences between the items or concepts. As students develop their compare and contrast essays, remind students that the specific points being compared and contrasted must be of the same type or class. For example, a student may have an assignment to compare and contrast vehicles used to carry passengers and camping equipment. To compare an SUV with a motorcycle would be impractical. More sensibly, this compare and contrast essay becomes viable when the vehicles being compared and contrasted actually possess the capability of meeting given criteria. Therefore, points of comparison and contrast in this essay might include a discussion of not only SUVs but also trucks equipped with crew cabs (a four- or six-passenger truck). Both of these types of vehicles can carry a load of sufficient size and carry passengers as well. The discussion for such an essay could then center around such categories or features as vehicle size, load capacity, passenger capacity, engine size relative to load size or vehicle weight, and comfort items such as air-conditioning, storage compartments, or a quality CD player. As to organizational structure, you could help students understand that they have three options to compare and contrast: subject by subject, point by point, or a combination of subject by subject and point by point. When comparing and contrasting subject by subject, students could discuss all of the features relating to, for example, Ford Expeditions and then all of the features relating to Chevrolet Suburbans, both comparable SUVs. When comparing and contrasting point by point, they could discuss feature by feature; that is, they could discuss the load capacity of the Expedition and then immediately discuss the load capacity of the Suburban.

Helping students: Because compare and contrast essays present a greater challenge, help students set up a chart that shows the specific elements being compared and contrasted. Create a column for the features being compared and contrasted and a column for each item being compared. Are the features being compared and contrasted of the same type? If not, brainstorm about the features. What features of the Expedition and the Suburban are the same? What features are different? If air-conditioning is an important feature in buying an SUV, then air-conditioning must be mentioned as a feature under both the Expedition and the Suburban.

A compare and contrast chart about Expeditions and Suburbans would look like this.

Features	Expedition	Suburban
Engine size	Student's point to be made about the engine size of the Expedition.	Student's point to be made about the engine size of the Suburban.
Passenger capacity	Student's point to be made about the passenger capacity of the Expedition.	Student's point to be made about the passenger capacity of the Suburban.
Load capacity	Student's point to be made about the load capacity of the Expedition.	Student's point to be made about the load capacity of the Suburban.
Air-conditioning	Student's point to be made about the air-conditioning of the Expedition.	Student's point to be made about the air-conditioning of the Suburban.
Ease of handling	Student's point to be made about the ease of handling of the Expedition.	Student's point to be made about the ease of handling of the Suburban.

Once students have identified the features to be discussed and have identified the similarities and differences, they can then decide on an organizational pattern of point by point, subject by subject, or a combination of point by point and subject by subject.

Cause and Effect

The cause-and-effect essay can be written from three different approaches. Students can discuss only causes, only effects, or both cause and effect. The key to effective cause-and-effect writing is for the essay to show the logical connection between the cause and the effect and to present the most relevant points so that a clear picture is presented. Cause-and-effect essays require writers to think deeply about the situation and to examine both the immediate and remote causes. A roof could collapse during a heavy snowstorm, but is the snow's weight the only cause of the collapse? Could poor building materials, faulty construction, faulty design, or not clearing the snow in a timely fashion also be contributing factors? Look for the logical connections, for all possible causes or effects, and for the method of presentation of the essay when you are helping students.

Helping students: If students are having difficulty with cause-and-effect essays, have them engage in a pre-writing exercise such as brainstorming to explore the causes and effects. Use questioning as a thought prompter. You might ask the student, "Is this the only cause or effect? What else could have caused this effect? What other effects do you think could possibly happen as a result of this cause? Could something in the past have caused this event or phenomena?" Students will begin to see their essays visually if they create a chart or list with three columns.

The Cause	The Event or Phenomena	The Effect of the Event or Phenomena

List the causes and effects under the appropriate heading. For example, a student brings in an essay addressing the question *What caused the increase in immigrants passing through Ellis Island in the year 1907 and what were the effects on the United States?* Because the prompt requires the student to look at both causes and effects, the chart might look like this.

The Causes: What caused people to migrate to the United States in 1907?	The Event	The Effect: What resulted from the increase of immigrants processed on Ellis Island?
Cause #1—student's reasons for the increase based on the student's readings	An increase in immigrants passing through Ellis Island in the year 1907	Effect #1—student supplied effects of the increase based on student's readings and class lectures.
Cause #2		Effect #2

Remember that most causes and effects are part of a "causal chain" where one or more causes lead to an effect and then that effect has an impact so that it now becomes the cause of other effects. This concept can be charted as follows.

Cause: People migrating to the United States produced a given **effect**: an increase in the number of people passing through Ellis Island. The increase in the people passing through Ellis Island created certain effects within the United States, so the increase in immigration became the cause that fostered other causes. The chain would look like this:

Cause → Effect → ↓

    Cause → Effect → ↓

        Cause → Effect → ↓

            and so on.

When you are conferencing with students on a cause-and-effect essay that looks at a chain of causes and effects, remind students that they will have to limit the scope of their essay if the chain can go on and on.

Rhetorical Mode Summary

The most crucial point to know about rhetorical modes is that they are tools, and rarely does a single rhetorical mode appear by itself; instead, they must work in concert with one another. Look at any classification essay, and you will find most of the other modes being used to prove the thesis of the essay. For instance, to classify means that writers must set up categories or classes. For the reader to understand the differences among classes, you may need to ask your tutee to define each class, to compare items in each class, and to explain each class, using detailed description or narration. In addition, the writer may need to show how each class is related one to another, or to show how one class logically leads to another.

As with any good writing, have students look to the audience, purpose, central idea, and methods of organization as you help these writers develop their essays.

Chapter 13

Helping Students with Research Papers

Although this guide provides insight into helping students with the basics of the writing process, you will also tutor more advanced students who already know how to develop an essay with an introduction, body paragraphs, and a conclusion, but they may need help on developing a research paper backed up by solid sources and documentation. In order to provide insight into conferencing on research papers, this chapter, through the use of dialogues, will focus on the research process and the tutor's role. This chapter will look at the following:

- helping the first time research writer: a dialogue
- suggestions for helping students during the research process
- moving the student from research to note-taking and avoiding plagiarism: a dialogue
- encouraging the student to write a first draft with audience, purpose, and a thesis
- reviewing the rough draft

The question *How do you help the student who is doing a research paper?* is a valid question because the scope of doing the research could span days, week, or months—a stretch of time that easily suggests that more than one tutoring session might be needed. Obviously, when the research is complete and the paper is in draft form, you can help the research student by using the same tools that you would help any student writing any other essay. Although the student may require assistance with in-text citations and the works cited, a student doing research may also come to a writing center in hopes that a tutor could help him or her

- understand the assignment itself
- develop a topic
- narrow a thesis

- grasp the concepts of developing an argumentative essay
- brainstorm methods of gathering information
- comprehend the methods of note-taking
- format in-text citations, footnotes, a works cited, or a bibliography
- formulate strategies needed to put the entire research project together

To give you a sense of how to help a student who is in the beginning stages of writing a research paper, this section will go through an initial contact between a tutor and "Mr. Freshman Comp" as he writes his first college research paper.

Helping Mr. Freshmen Comp, the First Time Research Writer: A Dialogue

As the neon lights flicker overhead, Mr. Freshman Comp (FC) walks into the writing center.

MR. FRESHMAN COMP: Yo, tutor; I have to write this research paper, and it's due in two weeks. My teacher assigned it two weeks ago, but I just didn't have time to start working on it. I need help, man. I've never done a paper like this one.

TUTOR: *(You smile and pull out a seat at the tutoring table.)* Two weeks?

FC: *(FC spreads his books and papers on the table and slides into the seat.)* Yup.

TUTOR: Well, what have you done so far?

FC: *(points to his open notebook)*

TUTOR: There's nothing there.

FC: That's what I've done.

TUTOR: Well, what have you learned about doing research so far?

FC: I need a topic and I need to narrow it.

TUTOR: Why don't you get out your pen and jot these things down? *(You wait.)*

FC: *(fumbles for a pen)* Is this enough paper?

TUTOR: Sure. Since I'm sure your teacher already covered these points, let's review the research process. In the next few days you need to accomplish these steps:
- Narrow your subject to a topic worth researching and a topic that interests you.
- Gather the information. That is, research the library and Internet to locate sources.
- Read the material and sort out which of your sources can support your thesis.
- Take notes on the information so that you can remember the important points. When you are taking notes, you can summarize, paraphrase, or quote directly what an author is

saying, and you should include notes that reflect your
reactions, opinions, and judgments as well as your reactions to
your reading. Also, note connections you see between the
various sources.
Am I going too fast?

FC: No. I remember going over this in class. Am I really supposed to
            write what I think of an article or how one article seems the same
            or different from another?

TUTOR: Yes, you should record your reactions. Remember, this is your
            research paper, your thesis, your topic sentences. In short, you are
            defending your opinion. So react to your research material while
            you are reading. Look for connections as well as identify
            weaknesses in arguments.

FC: Oh, yeah, I remember. . . (FC *fumbles through his notebook.*) I
            think I have a handout, ah . . . (FC *points to a section and begins to
            read from the handout.*) This handout says, "The steps you should
            take include selecting and narrowing the general topic . . ." I know,
            we said that . . . (FC *moves finger down the paragraph.*) ah,
            "Gather . . ." We said that. "Take notes . . ." uh . . . yes.

TUTOR: Perhaps I can help?

FC: (*looking at tutor*) No, I remember discussing this. Here it is. The
            handout says that I should do four things: "(1) Analyze and
            interpret the information gathered in research; (2) Think
            critically; (3) Produce a well-stated thesis statement; and (4)
            Support opinions, judgments, and conclusions by properly citing
            authorities."
            (*FC pauses and stares at the page.*)

TUTOR: Good, so let's . . .

FC: But, ah, I mean, where do we start?

TUTOR: Well, actually, you will start. I am here to merely help you. The
            best place to start, I think, is with step one—selecting and
            narrowing the topic. What topics interest you?

FC: Girls.

TUTOR: In your class.

FC: How about how the Americans helped win WWII?

TUTOR: How long did you say the paper had to be? When is it due?

FC: Topic too big?

TUTOR: Way too big, or as you teacher might say, your topic is too broad.
            What things interest you?

FC: Music.

TUTOR: What about music interests you?

FC: I like music videos.

TUTOR: What is in the music videos that you like?

FC: The . . . ah . . . I could write a paper on violence in the media.

TUTOR: Good idea, but how did you make that jump to violence in the
            media?

FC: We were discussing it in a class the other day. There's this cool article about how violence is impacting kids.

TUTOR: So, you know there are articles about violence in the media?

FC: Sure. I bet there are a bunch, so it would be easy to research.

TUTOR: But what is your position? I mean, how do you feel about violence.

FC: Oh, I think they are right.

TUTOR: But what is your position? For instance, is there too much violence on TV?

FC: You bet. You ought to see my little brother—karate chops everything in sight. And kids learn fast. I have this niece. She is only twenty months old, but she knows how to put a videotape in the VCR and punch on the TV.

TUTOR: How will violence on TV impact her?

FC: Oh, I think she'll pick it up real fast.

TUTOR: Well, what's the topic of your paper going to be?

FC: How violence on TV hurts kids.

TUTOR: Be more specific, and write your ideas in your notebook. Try two or three different topics. Be specific.

FC: (writes several sentences in his notebook) How about: Violence on TV impacts children in a negative way because it teaches them to use violence as a problem-solving method.

TUTOR: You were busy in those few minutes of writing. Where did you come up with violence as a problem-solving technique?

FC: Not technique, method. And I am not sure. It just came to me.

TUTOR: Well, let's work with that for now. Can you form that statement into a research question?

FC: Does violence on TV impact children in a negative way? Okay?

TUTOR: Okay. And your tentative answer to that question is what?

FC: That it does have a bad influence.

TUTOR: Good. As you do your research, try to answer your research question. You'll find that your research will either prove that your hypothesis is correct—that TV violence has a bad influence on children—or that your hypothesis needs to be modified or changed.

FC: So, I'm ready to go.

TUTOR: Before you leave, develop your own reasons why TV violence has a bad influence on kids. These reasons will be the main points that you need to show or prove as you present your argument. After you have a quick sketch of reasons why you think your thesis is true, you can go out and look for sources to support your position.

FC: Wow. Sounds like a lot of work, but I think I know three or four reasons right now.

TUTOR: Write your hypothesis down and beneath it list your reasons.

FC: (writes for a few minutes, looks up, returns to writing)

TUTOR: How you doing?

FC: Almost done. I'm on a roll.

TUTOR: Great. Now you're ready to do the research.

FC: Oh, you mean I'm ready to go source hunting.
TUTOR: Okay, where are you going to hunt?
FC: The library, the Internet.
TUTOR: Those are good places to start, but let's look at your handbook. Turn to the research section of your handbook.
FC: *(pulls out his handbook and opens to the research chapter)*
TUTOR: Read over the headings.
FC: Well, there's planning the research paper, and here's the research question. Here's an entire section on just the library. How could any one write that much about a library?
TUTOR: Let's look.
FC: *(turns to the section on the library)*
TUTOR: Notice that here is a discussion of the reference works you can find in the library, and here's a discussion of how to use the books and catalogs. Turn a few pages.
FC: *(turns a few pages)* What does it mean databases and CD-ROMs?
TUTOR: It is referring to databases such as InfoTrac or ProQuest on CD-ROM. Note also that you can get the *Reader's Guide to Periodical Literature* in a book or on CD. These are helpful, and the reference librarian can show you how to use them.
FC: I didn't realize there was so much in this handbook. Here's a section about online sources, with URLs and everything.
TUTOR: Your text on how to write the research paper has similar information, and so does the MLA handbook.
FC: I guess that I better look these over before I start.
TUTOR: A wise idea. But do go out on the Web, and do go to the library and talk to the research librarian to begin your adventure.
FC: Adventure?
TUTOR: Sure.
FC: You must be insane, pretty knowledgeable, but insane if you think research papers are an adventure.
TUTOR: Come see me when you've found your sources, and we'll see how insane it is. And don't forget to do your note cards.

In this tutoring session, the tutor was able to help the student review what he knew about the research paper, narrow a topic to a preliminary thesis statement, and review possible places for the student to do his research—his source hunting. When you tutor someone on this level, be sure to emphasize using the library and consulting the research librarian who is an expert on researching good sources.

Moving the Student from Research to Note Taking and Avoiding Plagiarism: A Dialogue

The dialogue continues with Mr. Freshman Comp coming back to see the tutor after he has located five sources.

FC: I've found all this stuff on the Internet. I think I have enough sources. (*spreading flat a piece of paper*) See, I have the five sources my instructor said I had to have. So let's start writing. I've only got till next week before it's due.

TUTOR: (*reviewing the bibliography*) Where's your notes cards?

FC: I jotted a few ideas down in this notebook, and I have these quotes. I have the paper worked out in my head. All I have to do is copy in my quotes, and I will be done.

TUTOR: So you want to be accused of plagiarism, to fail the assignment, and possibly to be kicked out of school?

FC: (*laughs*) That won't happen. I have my quotes. Isn't that enough?

TUTOR: Where did you get the material, the ideas, that you said are organized in your head?

FC: From my reading, of course.

TUTOR: Exactly.

FC: No, seriously. Look, all I do is take a quote and change a word here or there, and I don't have to cite it because it is not precisely what the author said.

TUTOR: Do you have your handbook or your textbook or even the handout you brought last time?

FC: I have this handbook and this textbook, *Writing With Good Cite: A Panoramic View of the Research Process.*

TUTOR: Let's look at the chapter in your textbook that talks about avoiding plagiarism. (*turns to the section discussing plagiarism*)

FC: (*reads for a moment*) Wow! Did you know that taking not only a writer's words, but also his or her ideas or organization is plagiarism?

TUTOR: That's right. Didn't your instructor mention something similar in class?

FC: I guess I better take some more notes.

TUTOR: (*picking up the five note cards FC had placed on the table*) And it might be good to note the point you are proving or discussing here. (*You point to the upper-left corner of the 3 x 5 note card.*)

FC: You mean one of the paragraph points?

TUTOR: Yes. That way, you can quickly organize your information because you have already sorted by main and subpoint.

FC: So, my note cards should record quotes, paraphrases, and summaries.

TUTOR: Just as shown here. (*You point to the page in the book.*)

FC: And I should write down my ideas and reactions the same way?

TUTOR:	Yes. A research paper is not a list of quotes held together by a few words. It's your ideas and thoughts supported by various sources.
FC:	That's why my teacher said that a quote might make an interesting hook, but it could never be my thesis.
TUTOR:	Good point.
FC:	And, my teacher said that I want to support my idea, not someone else's.
TUTOR:	Absolutely.
FC:	I've got to get going.
TUTOR:	See you in a few days . . . after you have finished your note-taking. Also, you should start organizing a written outline from those note cards, quotes, and ideas in your head.

As the above dialogue indicates, your job as a tutor is to nudge the student into using the resources he or she already has available. A student may believe that all he or she needs to do is come to the writing center and magically, a paper will emerge. You need to continually place the burden of learning, of doing the research, and of writing the paper on the shoulders of the student while you guide, encourage, and offer concrete suggestions.

Encourage the Student to Write a First Draft

Once the student has done adequate note-taking and has prepared a preliminary outline, you can help the student by encouraging him or her to focus on the audience, purpose of writing, and thesis. For instance, you might help in these ways:

- Brainstorm variations of the thesis to help narrow the scope. Tell the student that it is not necessary to have a "perfect" thesis statement at this point but to formulate one that will give direction to the paper—a central point.
- Discuss strategies to integrate quotes, paraphrases, and summaries by using signal phrases and in-text citations (or footnotes depending on the format required—such as MLA, APA, or *Chicago*).
- Sharpen or clarify the outline so it can be a stronger writing tool. Ask the student leading questions designed to reveal additional ideas, main points, and possible areas for modifications and deletions. Help the student strengthen the logical links between main points and the thesis. Have the student examine the support and examples to be sure that they support each main point.
- Discuss how the student can move from an outline to paragraphs to the essay.
- Suggest that the student spend several days writing the paper.
- Suggest that the student return to the writing center in a few days for another tutoring session to review a draft of the essay itself.

Reviewing the Rough Draft

Once the student has generated an outline and a rough draft, you can proceed in the same manner that you would with any essay. However, since this research paper includes drawing logical connections and inferences from the information provided as well as source citations, you may want to spend additional time on a few areas.

- Look for ways to revise the outline. If the student has done his or her homework, the outline will give you a quick overview so that you will know what to expect in the draft. It will also give a hint to weaknesses in logic or structure.
- Guide the student to write notes in the margins of his or her paper to determine the topic of each paragraph. If one paragraph covers more than one topic, then direct the student to create several paragraphs from the one paragraph.

As you read through the paper, you can do the following to help:

- Look for jumps in thought or logical development within a paragraph as well as jumps in thought from one paragraph to the next. The argument or discussion must flow logically. Often a student, however, becomes so involved in providing quotes, paraphrases, or summaries, that he or she forgets that this paper must develop a thesis and, therefore, must flow logically from idea to idea.
- Look for areas where the student is depending on quotes to make the point. This essay represents the student's thinking, so be sure that when the student draws on outside sources, he or she takes time to explain exactly how the outside sources show or prove the point that the student is making.
- Look for repetition of thought or redundancies of words, phrases, or clauses.
- Look for paragraphs that need topic sentences, topic sentence revision, or transitions added.
- Look for clarity of thought.
- Look for logical fallacies.

At the conclusion of this session, you might suggest to the writer that to produce a polished paper, several more rewrites are necessary. Then, the writer needs to, on his own, do another review of the paper looking at content, logic and organization; finally, the writer is ready to do an examination of grammar, punctuation, and the mechanics of the paper.

Chapter 14

Putting It All Together

You have now spent some time immersing yourself in thoughts behind how you will tutor your first students. You wonder what your first tutee will ask of you. Will a student bring in an essay that needs some minor organizational revision, will a student bring in a rough paper with many sentence level problems and lack of clarity, or will an ESL student bring in an essay that lacks articles and prepositions? In reality, you may have one or more of each type of student on your first day of tutoring.

You are now armed with knowledge about the art of tutoring, but is there a way that you can prepare for the first tutoring session without having to go "cold turkey"—sitting down and engaging in a tutoring session without actually having the experience?

Building Your Tutoring Confidence

You can build your tutoring confidence in several ways. You could consider the following:

- Engage in a few mock-tutoring sessions with your fellow tutors or with your supervisor. Use sample student essays provided by your writing center director, or use the ones provided in this chapter. Engage in a mock-tutoring session as if it were real. Think of possible opening remarks to the student. As you play act this type of session, practice so that you become accustomed to formulating leading questions and explanations that are meaningful but tactful.
- Shadow a more experienced tutor for a few tutoring sessions. Shadowing will let you hear ways that an experienced tutor greets students, phrases questions, and formulates different methods to encourage tutees to think, respond, and write.
- Engage in a "live" tutoring session but have an experienced tutor alongside you. In this way, the experienced tutor can help you if you "get stuck." This way may be more pressure filled because not only are you

tutoring a real student, but you have the more experienced tutor sitting with you. However, in this session, you will not feel that you are carrying the entire responsibility of the tutoring session.

- Use the dialogues presented in this guide as a source of reference to create your own tutoring scenarios. Have another tutor act the part of the student and respond differently than Tutee responded in these dialogues.
- Review the practices again. Try talking through the answers—verbalize the explanations. If it would help to make the exercise more real, play act with another tutor as you explain grammar concepts.

A Baker's Dozen: Ideas to Help Students Improve Essay Writing

As you tutor students on their essays remember to do the following:

1. Greet the tutee warmly and ask the tutee the class in which he or she is enrolled.
2. Ask the purpose of the essay.
3. Look for an introduction with a thesis statement if appropriate for the level of writing. Also, look for a thesis that is narrow enough.
4. Look for topic sentences and support with specific concrete details, examples, and illustrations.
5. Look for broad generalizations that need to be developed with support, examples, and sharpened commentary and discussion.
6. Look for unified paragraphs with no digression off the topic within a particular paragraph. As well, look for a unified introduction, body, and conclusion.
7. Look for logical flow from one idea to another with solid relationships between ideas through the use of transitional expressions or coordination.
8. Look for unnecessary redundancies, wordiness, or areas in need of improved clarity.
9. Look for ideas that need to be expressed more clearly because the point being made cannot be grasped by you or any other reader.
10. Look for structure based upon that mode, if a particular rhetorical mode should be present.
11. Look for a conclusion that summarizes the main points and ends with strength by using a suggestion, a call to action, or a look into the future.
12. Look for grammar and punctuation issues that need to be discussed with the writer.
13. Most importantly, look for areas to say "good job, "well written," and a way to encourage your tutee in his or her writing.

Below are three practice essays on which you may sharpen your tutoring skills. Use any of the methods mentioned above to engage in a practice session, hopefully with another person playing the part of the student writer.

Practice 25 Essay—The Basic Skills Writer

Practice your tutoring skills on the essay below. The student's essay is responding to a prompt to write at least three paragraphs about the theme of the novel *Chocolat* by Joanne Harris.

    The book Chocolate is a real good book. The book Chocolate by Joane Harris starts off with this mother Vianne and her daughter 6 year old Anouck and Pantoufle arriving at a town in France. Pantoufle is make-believe. They don't know anybody there. The town is having a Marti Grass carnival. The next day is Lent in the Catholic Church. I think the story is kind of about good and evil people and how the priest and some in the town don't like new people.

    Vianne and Anouck move into an old bakery and paint and clean it. Then the priest comes to talk. She tells him that she won't be going to the Catholic Church and he isn't too happy about that. Then the next chapter is kind of confusing. I dont think the author wanted you to know exactly who was in this chapter or understand because the story changes to the priest's story, he talks to someone else in this chapter and tells the other person all about Vianne. Then in the next chapter, it goes back to the story about Vianne, back and forth in each chapter for each day until Easter. Vianne plans this Easter chocolate festival that the priest and some people in town are against. But alot of the people in the town become Viannes friends and don't think that she is evil like the priest thinks.

    Well most of the story takes place in the bakery which is really a candy store. Vianne makes chocolates, cakes and hot chocolate. She can predict everyones favorite kind and is real generous. The priest does not want her to do this. He thinks shes a which and that shes evil. She makes lots of friends in the town anyway some people are nice to her and some people are on the priests side. There are lots of other characters in the story. Lots of people come into the store to buy candy. Most of the story is about other people. One guy he has a sick dog and the priest thinks he should put his dog to sleep. He comes in with his dog and talks to Vianne alot and Vianne talks to him and is his friend. Also its about Josephine. She has this husband who beats her and she runs away from him and the priest says that she is the wrong one because she broke the marriage vows. So Josephine moves into the candy shop and helps them and Vianne and Josephine become good friends. Also its about Armande an old lady who is Viannes friend but her daughter does not want her mother to be Viannes friend or eat what Vianne makes. Vianne liked Armande and they were friends. Vianne tried to help her because

Armandes grandson never gets to visit Armande because of his mother. So they met in the chocolate shop and they became friends and now Armande has a grandson. Most of the story was about Vianne and how she helps people. There is also the story about Roux and he comes to the town with all of the river boat people but some of the town doesnt like Roux or the other people because the town thinks they re dirty etc. Vianne becomes Roux's friend though. The priest was really against Roux and all his people on the riverboats. And then there is the story about the priest when he was small and he helps to burn down some other riverboats. So he is just as evil as anyone else but another priest forgives him. When the chapter is about Vianne she talks alot about her mother who died of cancer and how they travel alot all over the world and never settle down or own anything. Vianne is alot like her mother cause she and Anouk always travel to.

Mainly the story is about the priest who did not like her or the shop cause he thinks shes evil. But some of the village people came in anyway and they are her friends. Really it is the priest who is evil. He has been really hungry for all that chocolate all along. In the end on Easter Sunday morning the priest breaks into her shop and goes in the window and starts eating all the candy and she finds him. (Except that in the movie it was the mayor.) Then they all have a celebration. I would recommend the book to everyone to read.

Practice 26 The ESL Writer (whose writing level is several semesters below freshman composition)

Practice your tutoring skills on the essay below. The student's essay is responding to a prompt to write one paragraph about someone who is a hero.

My hero is president of United States George Bush. To day U.S.A. most mighty, powerfull, rich country in world and George Bush is first man of world. He is high educated, patient, courageous and firm man. The life gave him the very complex tasks and he solved them excellent. He has very skillfull and good assistants, counselors and others. They helped him solving problem U.S. inside and outside. Even when his enemies were trying to be terrorism, he for all his wisdom and courage takes care U.S. and other countries. He is ever one best presidents U.S.

Practice 27 Freshman Composition Level Essay

Practice your tutoring skills on the essay below. The student's essay is responding to a prompt to write a persuasive essay addressing the topic: Laws holding parents responsible for the crimes of their children are (are not) unreasonable—why or why not?

Today, teenagers commit lots of crime like grafitti, driving too fast, drinking, and other stuff. Sometimes some of the crimes that teenagers commit causes a loss of money so someone has to pay. The legislature is considering enacting laws that hold the teenager's parents responsible for the crimes of their children both financially and morally. But if the children are sixteen to eighteen years old, it would be an injustice to the parents if the law holds them responsible. It is also a disservice to the teen and to the community.

Teenagers at some point in their lives have to be held responsible for their actions. When a teenager reaches 16 years old and can drive, then the teenagers should be responsible, not the parents. They have to take responsibility when they get there drivers license and start to drive because they should be able to think like a mature adult and think what to do in a serious situation. One situation when a teenager should think like a mature adult is when some guy comes up beside you and wants to drag race. It is not good and you should not do this because other people get killed. If teenagers take the responsibility of driving, then they have the capability to determine right from wrong.

Sixteen to 18 year olds are almost adults so they should behave and think more like an adult. I have a cousin who is a teenager and his mom doesn't make him act very much like an adult. He likes to do grafitti on buildings and his mom always pays. She should not do this because my cousin is old enough to know that he is destroying other people's property. One time he painted the entire side of a building, and my aunt paid. My cousin should of paid for at least part of it. Since he can drive a car, he could get a job. He is old enough to be treated like an adult, so he is old enough to pay himself. His parents should not be the ones.

Some people by the time they are 18 years old are already married and some even have children so why should parents be responsible if they are old enough to get married? They are no longer in the control of there parent. Why should the parent be held liable for the actions of these adult children? These teenagers should pay for their own crimes they commit, not the parents.

Age makes a difference if the parents should be held responsible. Parents should control and be responsible for the things their young children do. If a 6-year-old steals something then the parents should be responsible and pay. If the child is 16 years old then the parents should know what is going on, but the teenager should be responsible and laws should not only hold the parents responsible because holding parents responsible for the crimes of their 16 to 18-year-old teen only encourages the teen to commit other crimes because it doesn't put the responsibility on the teenager. Therefore, laws should not hold the parents responsible but it depends on the age of their children.

* * * * *

Looking Ahead

- Depending on how your writing center is organized (whether it has walk-ins, appointments, or a combination), you may experience some free-time between tutoring sessions. During this free time, you might review your handbook, computer software, or this guide. In short, use your free time to sharpen your skills.
- Seek to be as professional as you can. Any professional spends as much time as possible sharpening his or her skills and keeping abreast of current trends in his or her areas of specialty. Tutoring is no different. Your goal is to be professional, to be effective for your tutees, and to be proud of yourself. Remember that your primary task is to become the best possible tutor you can be.

Answers to Practices

Practice 1 – Identifying Nouns, Pronouns, Main Verbs, and Auxiliary (Helping) Verbs

1. Lance Armstrong (N) has (AUX) written (MV) his (PRO) autobiography (N) Tour de France (N) his (PRO) battle (N) cancer (N)
2. Some (PRO) people (N) see (MV) Armstrong (N) hero (N)
3. Lance Armstrong (N) ice skater (N) Scott Hamilton (N) has (AUX) overcome (MV) cancer (N) continues (MV) his (PRO) sport (N)
4. They (PRO) have (AUX) demonstrated (MV) strength (N) willpower (N) adversity (N)
5. Armstrong (N) has (AUX) been (AUX) speaking (MV) groups (N) survival (N)

Practice 2 Identifying Prepositions and Prepositional Phrases

Prepositions in **bold**

1. (**During** the Depression), people tried to earn money (**by** selling an apple) (**for** five cents).
2. (**On** New Year's Eve) (**in** 1928), Americans were spending money (**without** a care), but (**by** New Year's Eve 1929), many Americans no longer felt the joy (**of** celebrating).
3. (**In** the Dust Bowl years), families packed suitcases (**with** all their necessary items), threw their few possessions (**in** the car), and took **off** (for California). [**Off** is a particle.]
4. (**For** a long time), people avoided saving money (**in** a bank) (**because of** the many bank failures) (**after** the Stock Market Crash) (**of** 1929).
5. However, today my parents have instilled (**in** me) the value (**of** saving money) (**in** a bank account).

Practice 3 Identification of Adjective and Adverbs

	Word	Part of Speech	Word Modified
1.	hurriedly	adverb	ran
	frantic	adjective	teacher
	copy	adjective	center
	final	adjective	exam
	inconveniently	adverb	misplaced
2.	yesterday	adverb	saw
	video	adjective	version
3.	many	adjective	people
	swashbuckling	adjective	movies
	skilled	adjective	fencer
	appealing	adjective	challenge
	intellectual	adjective	strategy
	athletic	adjective	endurance
	graceful	adjective	movement
4.	fencing	adjective	bout
	only	adverb	ten
	ten	adjective	minutes
	extremely	adverb	exhausting
5.	never	adverb	had seen
	Shakespearean	adjective	plays
	quite	adverb	so
	so	adverb	exuberant

Practice 4 Identifying Conjunctions

	Conjunction	Type of Conjunction
1.	neither . . . nor	correlative
2.	and	coordinating
	therefore	conjunctive adverb
3.	and	coordinating
4.	although	subordinating
	and	coordinating
5.	after	subordinating
	and	coordinating
6.	or	coordinating
	however	conjunctive adverb
	and	coordinating
7.	because	subordinating
8.	either . . . or	correlative
	and	coordinating
9.	yet	coordinating
10.	because	subordinating

Practice 5 Identifying Verbs and Verbals

	Verb	Verb Tense	Verbal	Type of Verbal
1.			ignored	participle
	chewed	simple past		
2.	is succeeding	present progressive		
			kicking	gerund
3.			sprinting	participle
	caught up	simple past		
4.	wants	simple present		
			to be	infinitive
5.	work	simple present		
			to find	infinitive
			causing	participle
6.			blazing	participle
	has been warming	present perfect progressive		
7.			working	participle
	will finish	simple future		
8.	had been hunting	past perfect progressive		
9.	had caused	past perfect		
			to seek	infinitive
10.			riding	gerund
	helps	simple present		
			to relax	infinitive

Practice 6 Passive Voice Versus Active Voice

Though answers may vary, possible revisions include:

1. Did the dealership repair the car?
2. The builder constructed the house in only five months.
3. Car emissions have polluted the earth's environment.
4. Samantha enjoyed an around-the-world trip during the summer.
5. During winter break, many students took Math 90 in only three weeks.

Practice 7 Identifying Subject, Verbs, and Prepositional Phrases

1. <u>Did</u> the <u>thunder</u> and <u>lightning</u> <u>scare</u> all the youngsters (at camp) (during the night)?
2. <u>Finish</u> the project before <u>you</u> <u>leave</u>. [*you* understood as the subject of *finish*]
3. Most <u>colleges</u> <u>have</u> fewer students (in attendance) (during the summer).
4. The <u>pond</u> <u>was frozen</u> and <u>had become</u> slippery (during the big ice storm).
5. (Across the horizon), the <u>hikers</u> <u>saw</u> the summit that <u>they</u> still <u>needed</u> to cross.

Practice 8 Subject–Verb Agreement

	Verb	**Subject to Agree with**
1.	gives	each
	vote	all
2.	ruin	viruses and worms
3.	is	printer
4.	tastes	coffee
5.	loves	everyone
6.	is	*Great Expectations*
7.	are	countries
8.	climb	both
9.	are	none
10.	attends	group

Practice 9 Pronoun Agreement

Other answers are possible.

1. Should ~~a~~ students revise their own essays, or should students take their essays to a learning center?
2. A penny saved is a penny earned; ~~that~~ **saving money** is something we should do.
3. The Hippie Movement began in the 1960's because ~~they~~ **hippies** rejected the "Establishment" and traditional American customs.
4. A slump in business activity may cause a recession, so this **slump** may cause the value of real estate to decline also.
5. Some people enjoy reading books on a hot summer day, and the library is a good place to find ~~them~~ **books**.
6. Each dancer hopes that during a performance, **he or she** will make all the right moves..
7. Did everyone come prepared with ~~their~~ **his or her** speech?
8. At the bank, when Mr. Wilson gave the man the money, ~~he~~ **the man** counted it two times.

9. We go to the block long mall often because we like ~~their~~ **its** stores and boutiques.
10. Each of the members must do ~~their~~ **his or her** part on the committees.

Practice 10 Identifying Types of Phrases

      infinitive – subject   infinitive – subj complement
1. <u>To be able to write well</u> is <u>to be able to communicate</u>.

   gerund – subject   gerund – subject   gerund – subject
2. <u>Planning the plot</u>, <u>developing the characters</u>, and <u>creating the setting</u> of a novel takes time and patience.

                     appositive
3. Oprah Winfrey's Book Club, <u>a phenomenal success</u>, has encouraged

gerund – direct obj   appositive
<u>reading of books</u>, <u>both</u> <u>modern and classical</u>.

        gerund – subject
4. <u>Reading books while on vacation</u> is enjoyable.

           infinitive – direct obj.
5. Kevin plans <u>to read all the Harry Potter books</u>.

            gerund – object of prep
6. Lin plans on <u>reading *The Lord of the Rings* trilogy</u> this summer.

                  gerund – subject
7. The members of my family think that <u>reading as many books as they can</u> is valuable.

             infinitive – direct obj
8. Every emerging novelist wants <u>to write the great American novel</u>.

      appositive
9. The professor, <u>a witty man</u>, wrote two humor books when he retired.

      participial
10. Manuscripts <u>typed on a word processor</u> look better than manuscripts

      participial
<u>typed on an old-fashioned typewriter</u>.

Practice 11 Identifying Types of Clauses

1. no subordinate clause

   Adverb
2. <u>After the boy ate lunch</u>, he went swimming.

Adverb   adjective
3. When he went swimming, the boy who was unfamiliar with the lake
    went into the deep part.

                      adverb
4. Leah, because she wanted to impress Colin, purchased a new dress;

                          adverb
    however, when she tried it on for her mother, her mother did not
    approve of the dress.

                noun
5. What he wanted to say was not allowed.

                      noun
6. She feared that the time was up.

                          adverb
7. Leave the money where no one will find it.

                                              noun
8. He didn't know anything about the crime except what the newspapers
    reported.

9. From a little after 11:00 A.M. until almost 5:00 P.M., the jurors sat in what

                        noun   *adverb cl* **subject**
    all of them felt was a cramped sequester room because the judge,

                adjective   *adverb cl*   **verb**
    who was a stickler for following rules, did not want the jury approached

                    adjective
    by anyone who might be a media reporter.

                              adjective
10. The Beach Boys, who started singing in the 1960's, still perform at

                      adjective
    concerts where people of all ages enjoy their music.

                            noun
11. You might think that this is a simple sentence, but it is not.

12. No subordinate clause

                    adverb
13. Although my family thinks otherwise, I am a good cook.

                    adverb
14. Since complex sentences are interesting, we write many of them.

                                              noun
15. The meaning of the ambiguous reference is whatever the reader wants to
    make of it.

Practice 12 Identification of Sentence Types

1. simple
2. complex
3. compound
4. compound-complex
5. compound-complex
6. compound
7. compound-complex
8. simple
9. complex
10. complex

Practice 13 Sentence Combining and Identification

Answers may vary; possible answers include:

1. Megan's old car was put to shame when she saw her friend's restored 1968 Mustang that had a new blue paint job. [complex]
2. Because the car's engine blew up, the mechanics shop repaired the car's engine. [complex]
3. The ants crawled into the house and appeared in the bedroom; consequently, the bedroom had to be sprayed for ants. [compound]
4. April in Paris is beautiful, so tourists, who love to go there, visit the Eiffel Tower. [compound-complex]
5. A lightening strike started the brush fire that roared through the hills and burned over 10,000 acres in one day. [complex]
6. When the large ship pulled into port yesterday, the passengers got off for two hours and shopped in the tourist district. [complex]
7. Some might say that people with recognizable Hollywood names influence California politics; for example, Ronald Reagan was governor of California, Sonny Bono was mayor of Palm Springs, Clint Eastwood was mayor of Carmel, and Arnold Schwarzenegger is governor of California. [compound]
8. While many people listen to rock music, county music is also popular; in addition, young people like rap music and hip-hop too.   [compound-complex]
9. Peggy Sue loved the song that was played on a guitar and sung by a rising county-rock star. [complex]
10. After the communist regime ended in 1989, the Berlin Wall came down; Bonn had been West Germany's capital, and now Berlin is the capital of the unified country. [compound-complex]

Practice 14 Identification and Repair of Fragments, Comma Splices, and Run-on Sentences

Sentence repairs may vary.

1. [fragment] The saying "all's well that ends well" is also the title of a Shakespearean play.

2. [run-on] The Greeks won the Trojan War when they constructed an enormous hollow horse. **It** became known as the Trojan Horse.
3. [comma splice] In their trick, the Greeks claimed that the horse was a gift to honor the goddess Athena**;** however**,** the Greeks hid inside to sneak out later and sack Troy.
4. [run-on] Can you come to the beach today**,** or can you come tomorrow?
5. [fragment] The firefighters **were racing** down the street to make a rescue.
6. [fragment] On top of the burning building **a man was** standing ready to jump.
7. [comma splice] The firefighters climbed up the ladder**;** then, they carried the man down.
8. [comma splice] Everyone on the ground cheered **because** the firefighters were heroes.
9. [fragment] The man's family **was** thankful for Engine Company 98.
10. [run-on] Later Engine Company 98 had a special dinner **where** the heroes were honored.
11. [fragment] The Smithsonian exhibits the collection of inaugural gowns **worn** by the First Ladies.
12. [correct]

Practice 15 Repair of Misplaced or Dangling Modifiers

1. The elephant **that weighed three tons** walked over the man.
2. After driving all night, **Ed and Tom** finally pulled into a motel.
3. Sherrie practiced the piano for **almost** twenty minutes.
4. Tanning her body, **Pam said that** the sun felt good.
5. Skiing down the slope, **he almost crashed into a tree**.
6. He went **nearly** twenty-five yards before he saw the tree.
7. To avoid the tree, **the man veered** his skis to the right.
8. The man rolled down **approximately** two hundred feet of the snow slope.
9. Trying to look in the window, the boy **who was barely four feet tall** saw the little truck.
10. Put the dress **that has been altered** in the box.

Practice 16 Repair of Shifts

Several different repairs are possible.

Known as the "cowboy artist," Charles M. Russell was born in 1865. Having lived in the West during the last half of the nineteenth century and early twentieth century, he **saw** the West of the great cattle drives and the country where Lewis and Clark **went** up the Missouri River. As an artist of the Old West, Russell visualized for **people** what no words could express. One of his most famous sketches **is** "The Last of the Five Thousand" that **depicts** the winter of 1886–1887 when thousands of cattle **died** in the freezing weather.

His sketch **shows** the effect that the cold winter **had** on the cattle industry in Montana. Charles Russell also **painted** or **sketched** pictures of the American Indian. One of his paintings **depicts** the Lewis and Clark Expedition led by Sacajawea when the group **met** the Flathead Indians in the Bitterroot Mountains. Russell also was an illustrator for calendars and magazines, but today he is best known for his large scale paintings that **illustrate** the Old West.

Practice 17 Repairing Sentences for Clarity and Flow

Answers may vary. One possible revision:

The Cherokee Indians were one of the first Native American tribes to be known as a "civilized" tribe. In the early 1800's, some Cherokees felt that they needed to live more like the white people to survive and to retain their ancestral homelands in the Southeast United States. To help in this "civilization" process, mixed-ancestry Cherokee leaders invited white people into their nation to help educate Cherokee children. Additionally, the United States government encouraged missionaries from the New England states to travel to the Cherokee Nation where they established schools. Many Cherokee children were educated at these boarding schools where they learned the English language. Boys learned about agriculture, and girls learned domestic skills such as sewing, spinning yarn, and cooking. Also, the Cherokees were known as a "civilized" tribe because Sequoyah, a Cherokee who could not read English, invented a syllabary for the Cherokee language. On leaves, he wrote down symbols that became the eighty-six symbols of the Cherokee syllabary; some looked like the English alphabet and some looked like Greek letters. Sequoyah's syllabary was introduced to the Cherokees who were then able to learn to read and write in a matter of weeks. After the *Cherokee Phoenix* was first published in 1828, Cherokees could now read in their own language the news of their nation, read about Cherokee laws, and read about people in other parts of the United States. Though there are several reasons why the Cherokees became known as a "civilized" tribe, the education of Cherokee children and the invention of the Cherokee syllabary contributed directly to their "civilization."

Practice 18 Repair of Punctuation and Mechanical Errors

1. Melissa saved **eight hundred dollars** in **six** months; therefore, she had enough money to buy the dining room set.
2. After his release from prison, Nelson Mandela was elected President of South Africa, and he also won a Nobel Peace Prize.
3. On June 13, 2003, the family will have an engagement party.
4. It never snows in Death Valley. **It** gets scorching hot in the summer.
5. Arlene said, "It's so cold; please close the door."

6. Do you want to help in the food line, or do you want to hand out blankets?
7. Sydney, when he is tired, will rest only in the comfort of a snugly chair.
8. He will, however, sleep on a bed at night.
9. Cats, unlike dogs, are independent.
10. Adverbs can modify verbs, adjectives, or other adverbs.

Practice 19 Words Often Confused and Words to Avoid

Today, **there** are **many** popular clubs to which car enthusiasts belong. One kind is the Early Ford V-8 Club. **Its** members own Fords built between 1932 and 1953. **Another** one is the Mustang Club **where its** members own classic Mustangs. The **effect** of having popular car clubs is that old Fords are now being restored **where** in years past, **many** cars were sold to wrecking yards. These clubs provide a social outlet for **their** members **too. Clubs may hold events such as** ice cream socials, classic car nights, or day trips in caravans. The only **drawback** about owning a classic car is the difficulty of finding parts to repair the old cars; however, belonging to a car club and meeting other owners helps when **club members** need to locate car parts.

Practice 20 Idiomatic Expressions [1]

1. **Give it a whirl** means to make a brief or experimental try.
2. **Keep up with the Joneses** means to match the lifestyle of wealthier neighbors or acquaintances.
3. **Trip down memory lane** means to remember a series of past life experiences.
4. **The odds are stacked against** means chances are poor as in the chances of winning.
5. **Strike while the iron is hot** means to take advantage of favorable conditions.

Practice 21 Use of Articles

1. What does no Rhonda do? She is an English teacher.
2. no dogs hate no cats.
3. The Giants lost to the Dodgers.
4. The State of California is having no economic problems.
5. no young people come to the United States to get an education.
6. The United Nations is an international organization.
7. The Pilgrims planned a feast to celebrate their survival in the colony at no Plymouth.
8. no people traveling on an airplane should plan on arriving at the airport two to two and a half hours before the time of no departure.

Practice 22 Prepositions – Free and Bound

All the prepositions are free prepositions except for the ones so indicated as bound.

During the years 1892 to 1924, when immigrants arrived in the United States, many of them passed through (**bound**) Ellis Island. Because of (**bound**) it historical significance, today Ellis Island is a historical landmark and part of the Statue of Liberty National Monument. People are interested in (**bound**) their roots, so millions of visitors a year travel there to look at (**bound**) where their ancestors first got off (**bound**) a ship to see the land of freedom and opportunity. These ancestors saw the United States as a place to start over (**bound**) to put down (**bound**) roots.

It wasn't until 1890 that Ellis Island was selected by the Federal government as the location for immigrants to enter the United States through the New York port. The immigration station formally opened on January 1, 1892. According to (**bound**) the official Ellis Island Web site, immigration was steady during the next few years and peaked in 1907 when, on a single day, 11,747 immigrants were processed on Ellis Island. Immigrants continued to arrive until 1924 when immigration started to drop off. (**bound**)

Practice 23 Use of Correct Modals

1. could
2. may
3. should
4. will
5. must
6. would

Practice 24 Analyzing Thesis Statements

1. It lacks an opinion or judgment that is narrow enough to discuss. Statement is dead end and lacks direction—what is *nice*?
2. The topic suggests an opinion or judgment and is narrow. The statement poses a question that demands an answer. It indicates a compare and contrast essay and indicates the possible content of the essay. If the assignment limited the word count or number of pages, further refinement may be needed to reduce the scope so a discussion could be accomplished within the specific word or page count.
3. The topic suggests an opinion and is narrow. The thesis provides a specific direction for the essay. The reader will look for a discussion of the humor of both the character and the author. As in question #2 above, further narrowing would be required to fit the length of the required assignment.
4. The topic shows direction and a specific opinion. It is narrow and will lead to a discussion of social customs and women's roles in a specific time

and culture. The shortcoming of this thesis is that much discussion might be required to explain social customs of King Arthur's time. The topic may fit a long essay or a research paper. However, for short essays, the writer may want to focus on one custom or aspect of LeFey's character.

5. There is no suggested opinion or judgment; the topic is not narrowed, but dead end.
6. Topic suggests no opinion or judgment; it is only a specific fact about Robert E. Lee.
7. Statement does not pose a question that demands an answer; it poses no opinion or judgment.
8. Statement is only a specific fact; it poses no opinion or judgment; no question is asked.
9. This is a statement only; there is no opinion or judgment; no question is posed.
10. This statement is narrow and suggests a opinion or judgment and poses a specific question. It poses a specific direction for the essay.

Practice 25 Essay—The Basic Skills Writer

Answers may vary.

Practice 26 The ESL Writer (whose writing level is several semesters below freshman composition)

Answers may vary.

Practice 27 Freshman Composition Level Essay

Answers may vary.

Notes

Chapter 1

[1] Many other books are available to help advanced writers improve tone and style. Among these books is the classic, *The Elements of Style* by William Strunk, Jr. and E. B. White, (Boston: Allyn and Bacon, 2000). Also see: John R. Trimble, *Writing with Style* (Upper Saddle River, N.J.: Prentice Hall Inc., 2000); and Joseph M. Williams, *Style: Ten Lessons in Clarity and Grace* (New York: Longman, 2002).

Chapter 2

[1] Beth Rapp Young, "Can You Proofread This?" in *A Tutor's Guide*, ed. Ben Raforth (Portsmouth, NH: Boynton/Cook Publishers, 2000), 113.

[2] William J. Macauley, Jr., "Setting the Agenda for the Next 30 Minutes," in *A Tutor's Guide*, 4.

[3] Molly Wingate, "What Line? I Didn't See Any Line," in *A Tutor's Guide*, 12.

[4] Stephen M. North, "The Idea of A Writing Center," in *The St. Martin's Sourcebook for Writing Tutors*, ed. Christina Murphy and Steve Sherwood (New York: Bedford/St. Martin's, 1995), 27.

[5] Ibid.

Chapter 4

[1] Ann Raimes, *Keys for Writers*, (Boston: Houghton Mifflin, 2005), 344; Raimes, *Universal Keys for Writers* (Boston: Houghton Mifflin, 2004), 423.

Chapter 6

[1] Edgar V. Roberts, *Writing about Literature* (Englewood Cliffs, N.J.: Prentice Hall, 1995), 263.

Chapter 8

[1] Concerning ESL writers, see *Keys for Writers* Supplementary Material by Naomi A. Sofer, and Ann Raimes, "Language Transfers: Tip Sheets for Ten Languages." *Instructor's Support Package* (Boston: Houghton Mifflin, 2005. Also see Ann Raimes, "Language Guide to Transfer Errors," *Universal Keys for Writers* (Boston: Houghton Mifflin 2004), 643–648; Ann Raimes, "Language Guide to Transfer Errors," *Keys for Writers* (Boston: Houghton Mifflin, 2005), 428; *Longman Advanced American Dictionary*, (Essex, England: Longman/ Pearson Education Ltd., 2001); and Leigh Ryan, *Bedford Guide for Writing Center Tutors* (New York: Bedford/St. Martins, 2002), 46.

[2] See Betty Schrampfer Azar, *Fundamentals of English Grammar* (New York: Longman, 2002); Irene E Schoenber, Marjorie Fuchs, Miriam Westheimer, Margaret Bonner, and Jay Mauer, *Focus on Grammar Series: Basic through Advanced* (New York: Addison Wesley, Longman, 1999-2000); Ann Raimes, *Keys for Writers;* Diana Hacker, *A Writer's Reference* (New York: Bedford/St. Martin's, 2003); and dictionaries such as *The American Heritage English as a Second Language Dictionary, Longman Advanced American Dictionary* or *Heinle's Newbury House Dictionary of American English.*

[3] "Ellis Island History," *Ellis Island Immigration Museum*, National Park Service, United States Department of the Interior, 2002. 31 Jul. 2003. <http://www.ellisisland.com/ history.html>.

[4] Some instructors include *ought to* and *have to* as modals.

Chapter 9

[1] *Zero draft writing* was a term used by Donald Murray in an early version of his article "The Maker's Eye" which has appeared in many college readers. More recently, John R. Trimble in his book *Writing with Style* used this term when he defines *zero draft* as his ". . . term for a throwaway—a piece of freewriting that allows you to warm up, get into the flow, work past your inhibitions, bust through your writer's block, etc."

Chapter 12

[1] Simpson, George, "The War Room at Bellevue," *New York Magazine*, 1983. Reprint in *Patterns of Exposition*, ed. Robert A. Schwegler. (New York: Longman/Addison-Wesley, 2001), 439.

[2] *The American Heritage Dictionary of the English Language* (New York: Houghton Mifflin, 2002), 1346.

Answers to Practices

[1] Meanings derived from *The American Heritage Dictionary of Idioms* or *Longman's Advanced American Dictionary*.

Suggested Reading and Bibliography

Sources on Writing Center Tutoring

Capossela, Toni-Lee. *The Harcourt Brace Guide to Peer Tutoring*. Fort Worth, TX: Harcourt Brace College Publishers, 1998.

Gillespie, Paula, and Neal Lerner. *The Allyn and Bacon Guide to Peer Tutoring*. Boston: Allyn and Bacon, 2000.

Murphy, Christina, and Steve Sherwood. *The St. Martin's Source Book for Writing Tutors*. New York: St. Martin's Press, 1995.

Rafoth, Ben, ed. *A Tutor's Guide: Helping Writers One to One*. Portsmouth, N.H.: Boynton/Cook Publishers, 2000.

Ryan, Leigh. *The Bedford Guide for Writing Tutors*. Boston: St. Martin's Press, 2002. [This book has an excellent annotated bibliography.]

The Writing Center Journal. International Writing Centers Association.

Writing Lab Newsletter. International Writing Center Association.

Sources for English Grammar and Writing

Azar, Betty Schrampfer. *Fundamentals of English Grammar*. 3rd ed. New York: Longman, 2002.

Fowler, H. Ramsey, and Jane E. Aaron. *The Little, Brown Handbook*. 8th ed. New York: Longman, 2002.

Gibaldi, Joseph. *MLA Handbook for Writers of Research Papers*. 6th ed. New York: Modern Language Association, 2003.

Hacker, Diana. *A Writer's Reference*. 5th ed. New York: Bedford/St. Martin's, 2003.

Hodges, John C., et al. *Hodges' Harbrace Handbook*. 15th ed. Fort Worth: Harcourt College Publishers, 2004.

Master, Peter Antony. *Systems in English Grammar: An Introduction for English Teachers*. Englewood Cliffs, New Jersey: Prentice-Hall, 1996.

Raimes, Ann. *Keys for Writers: A Brief Handbook*. 4th ed. Boston: Houghton Mifflin, 2005.

————. *Universal Keys for Writers*. Boston: Houghton Mifflin, 2004.

Roberts, Edgar V. *Writing About Literature*. 8th ed. Englewood Cliffs, New Jersey: Prentice Hall, 1995.

Schoenber, Irene E., Marjorie Fuchs, Miriam Westheimer, Margaret Bonner, Jay Mauer. *Focus on Grammar Series*: Basic through Advanced Levels. New York: Addison Wesley, Longman, 1999-2000.

Strunk, William Jr., and E. B. White. *The Elements of Style*. Boston: Allyn and Bacon, 2000.

Trimble, John R. *Writing with Style: Conversations on the Art of Writing*. 2nd ed. Upper Saddle River New Jersey: Prentice Hall, 2000.

Williams, Jospeh M. *Style: Ten Lessons in Clarity and Grace*. 7th ed. New York: Longman, 2002.

Suggested Dictionaries for ESL Use

The American Heritage English as a Second Language Dictionary. Boston: Houghton Mifflin, 1998.

The American Heritage Dictionary of Idioms for Students of English. Boston: Houghton Mifflin, 2001.

Heinle's Newbury House Dictionary of American English, Philip M. Rideout ed. 4th ed. Boston: Heinle Publishers, 1996.

Longman Advanced American Dictionary. Essex, England: Longman/Pearson Education Ltd., 2001.

Online Sources

A Writer's Reference companion web site: <dianahacker.com/writersref> [grammar explanations, drills, writing help, and exercises].

Community Colleges of Connecticut web site: <http://cc.comnetedu/grammar> [grammar explanations, drills, and quizzes].

Modern Language Association web site: <www.mla.org/> [bibliography, style guides, and resources].

Purdue University Online Writing Lab web site: <http://owl.english.purdue. edu> [grammar explanation, drills, and research paper help].

Universal Keys for Writers web site: <http://college.hmco.com/keys.html> [tutorials, documentation styles, web links, ESL center; also self-quizzes, eLibrary of exercises and an Internet Research Guide].

Index